STORIES *from the* GAME *of* LIFE

BOB WELCH

HARVEST HOUSE PUBLISHERS
Eugene, Oregon 97402

Cover design by Left Coast Design, Portland, Oregon

STORIES FROM THE GAME OF LIFE
Copyright © 2000 by Bob Welch
Published by Harvest House Publishers
Eugene, Oregon 97402

Library of Congress Cataloging-in-Publication Data
  Welch, Bob, 1954-
    Stories from the game of life / Bob Welch.
      p. cm.
    ISBN 0-7369-0265-1
      1. Christian life.   2. Athletes—Religious life.   3. Sports spectators—Religious life.   4. Sports—Religious aspect—Christianity. I. Title.

BV4596.A8 W45 2000
248.8'8—dc21   99—059681

Printed in the United States of America.

        00 01 02 03 04 05 06 07 08 09 / BP / 10 9 8 7 6 5 4 3 2

To my mother, Marolyn,
who never stopped cheering for me
and never stopped challenging herself

ACKNOWLEDGMENTS

With deep appreciation to:

— Ann Petersen, Greg Scandrett, Dan Roberts, and Nancy Shattuck-Smallwood, who read the initial manuscript and set the bar so high.

— Steve Panter, who allowed me to share his story, and his wife, Jan, who's the quiet encouragement behind that story.

— Ann and Jason Schar, whose laughter and love helped sustain me down homestretch.

— Tom Jordan, whose book, *Pre*, provided background for the chapter on runner Steve Prefontaine.

— My older son, Ryan, whose passion for sports—and life—inspires me.

— My younger son, Jason, whose last-inning heroics encourage me to never give up.

— My wife, Sally, whose patience with me and my writing often goes extra innings.

— My late father, Warren, who used to paint my boyhood football helmets with whatever team design I wanted (including those really difficult Rams horns).

— My Heavenly Father, who has blessed my life with such wonderful people.

Contents

From the Author

When I was 11, I won the "Beaver Huddle Armchair Quarterback Contest," meaning I was the entrant closest to predicting the score of the Oregon State-Syracuse football game. As a prize, I received a brown and white, regulation-sized football autographed by the entire 1965 Oregon State football team. I proudly placed that football on my bedroom shelf and vowed it would stay there forever.

A week later, that ball was so scuffed you couldn't read a name on it if you'd been Inspector Clouseau himself.

That's because after only a few days, I realized letting a football gather dust on a shelf made no more sense than leaving Silly Putty untouched in its plastic shell or keeping a dog cooped up in a pen. It was just plain wrong.

So I invited a bunch of friends over for street football and, together, we set that football free, doing with it what you're supposed to do with a football: we ran, lateraled, intercepted, punted, passed, and kicked it up and down Norwood Street for an entire afternoon, obliterating the names of Pete Pifer, Jack "Mad Dog" O'Bilovich, and all the other players in the process, but rationalizing that, as football players, they would understand.

This book is the literary equivalent of that football—the setting free of all sorts of thoughts on sports and life and dreams and death that have been gathering dust on my mind's shelf for much too long. And, as readers, you're like those friends I invited over to enjoy whatever memories, imagination, and insight this gift might unlock in us all.

Sports have played a huge part in our family, which consists of my wife, Sally, and our two sons, Ryan, now 20, and Jason, 17. But I'm a strange breed of sports aficionado. I'm not the guy sitting through three NFL games on a Sunday. I can't name a dozen current major league baseball players. And I'm so tired of spoiled millionaire athletes that, after the 1998-99 NBA strike, I silently protested by not watching a single shot on TV when play resumed.

But I've loved sports since I was young; among my most vivid memories of a once-in-a-lifetime family vacation to southern California was stopping at the famous Hearst Castle and being totally bored by all the architectural extravagance except for one thing: a poolside tile pattern that looked just like a baseball diamond. And just recently, I wound up in South Bend, Indiana, late one night but refused to even check into my hotel until I'd walked completely around hallowed Notre Dame Stadium, where I could almost hear Knute Rockne exhorting the boys to win one for the Gipper.

I've experienced sports as a sports editor, coach, referee, scorekeeper, fan, father, and athlete. (Well, not a real athlete; more like the agony-of-defeat guy who used to slide off the edge of the ski jump every Saturday afternoon on "ABC's Wide World of Sports.")

I've interviewed, in person, such athletes as Arnold Palmer, Dan Marino, Steve Largent, Peter Jacobsen, and Alberto Salazar, at one time the greatest marathon runner in the world. I've eaten breakfast with author and Walter-Mitty-of-sports George Plimpton, and lunched with Olympic gold medalist Dick Fosbury. I've covered Final Four basketball tournaments, played Pebble Beach twice, run two marathons, watched the final round of the PGA, written stories from the Orange Bowl press box, and been published in

Sports Illustrated. I saw Ken Griffey Jr. hit his first major-league home run and saw the late Steve Prefontaine run his final race, only hours before his death.

And yet what intrigues me most about sports has less to do with famous athletes than with the fascination of athletes of all abilities creating something from nothing; less to do with get-rich contracts than with deep-down character; less to do with the headlines than with the heart.

In particular, I'm intrigued by sports as a microcosm of life itself, the ebbs and flows of, say, a soccer game mirroring the ebbs and flows of our day-to-day existence.

Sports is a canvas on which athletes, as artists, create new works each day, no two alike.

It's a classroom in which the lessons of life are learned, the truth of God's wisdom played out.

It's a meeting place in which people draw near to one another, sometimes by identifying with a hero or team; sometimes by learning the value of teamwork; sometimes by realizing, as do some fathers and sons, that sports is one of the few things the two might have in common—not an end in itself, necessarily, but an entry to a deeper place.

While in Orlando, Florida, recently for a book publishing convention, I noted guests who hurriedly came and went, lost in their own little worlds, seemingly oblivious to one another. But when the U.S. women's soccer team began its quest to beat China in the World Cup championships, people gathered around the lobby TV like moths to a flame. Soon, these strangers were cheering with one another, commiserating with one another, connecting with one another with an almost-instantaneous sense of oneness.

Sports does that. I can't tell you how much money my late father made per year or how much our carpet cost per foot. But 35 years later, I can still remember playing knee football with that man on the living room rug on Sunday nights after *Lassie*.

I can't remember whether our first car was a V-6 or a V-8, but I remember the day Sally, then my wife of two years, subbed for the youth baseball team I coached. I remember the snickers when she stepped to the plate, the sudden quiet when she ripped a double to right-center, and the pitcher softly saying "Wow."

I can't remember a single purchase I made in the year 1995 but I remember, with great clarity, the way the sun broke through the early morning haze as my son Ryan and I golfed our way down the Oregon coast on a 7-mile-long hole we'd created.

Not that sports is sanctified with some sort of innate goodness or is superior to music or art or camping or anything else as a way of infusing our lives with meaning. Anyone who's seen a Little League parent go ballistic or remembers the Tonya Harding-Nancy Kerrigan ice skating incident has seen the ugly side of sports, of which there are many.

Still, sports remains one of the arenas in which lives are shaped, courage is tested, faith is steeled. In an ever-changing world, it's a place of permanence; "The National Anthem" is always sung before a game, stilling your soul for just a few moments that border on the sacred.

It's a place where tradition is still revered; at a Seattle-area paper where I once worked, the publisher would walk into the newsroom one day each April and throw out the "opening pitch" of the major-league baseball season.

It's a place laced with earthy ambiance; a withered hot dog that might make you nauseous if eaten at a convenience store would, if eaten at a baseball stadium, taste stunning.

Such is the way of sports. One June evening, just at dusk, I was aboard a jet as it descended to Dallas-Fort Worth International Airport. As I looked below, one thing stood out in the miles and miles of city and suburbia: dozens of lighted baseball diamonds that dotted the night like fireflies.

As I looked, I thought of all the baseball games being played all over America at that very moment: all the parents wanting so desperately to see their children succeed. All the coaches plotting strategy from their third-base boxes. All the players holding on to their secret dreams—to make the major leagues...to make All-Stars...to simply make it to first base any way they could...

Those of us smitten with sports are like the people at all those baseball fields: we each see the game from a different perspective, hold fast to different memories, and cling to different dreams.

What binds us together is that, like an impatient 11-year-old, we just can't let that autographed ball gather dust on the shelf.

The Athlete

❖ ❖ ❖

On the athletic stage, they are the ones in the spotlight. They train, practice, polish, and perform. They win a few and lose a few. They huff and puff and sweat and struggle. They dream of greatness and yet settle for something less. Usually. Every now and then, it all comes together and they live those dreams. They are the athletes.

Field of Dreams

I was doing some garage-sale pricing, going through all that leftover stuff of life that Sally and I were only too glad to sell to someone else, when I came upon it: an Atlanta Braves hat that looked decidedly small, as if it could fit on one of those spring-loaded, bouncing-head dolls that you used to see in the rear windows of cars.

"Whatayathink, twenty-five cents?" she said.

I barely heard her. Because when I saw that hat, I was back in the early '90s, in our backyard, firing a Wiffle ball to a 10-year-old son wearing that hat, a kid whose nickname was Rosebud because, like Ted Williams, he had a tendency to yank everything down the right-field line, the foul territory of which consisted of his mother's rose bushes.

Now when I say right-field line you need to visualize a left-field line because—well, because like most neighborhood baseball leagues, the Backyard Baseball Association (BBA) was not exactly conventional.

The league was founded in the early '90s, the creation of my two sons, 11 and 8 at the time, and a couple of their pals of similar ages. Among their first decisions was that first base would be located at what we traditionally think of as third base. Why? Because our rectangular backyard—not much bigger than a doubles tennis court—was situated in such a way that were you to overrun first base in its traditional location, you would smash into the right-field fence, which was only about five feet beyond the bag.

(Over the years, this reverse-direction motif worked well, the only hitch coming after Michael Jenson, one of Jason's pals and a kid on my Kidsports baseball team, once spent the night. The boys played BBA for about four hours that evening. The next morning, in a Kidsports game, Michael stepped to the plate, drove a single through the infield and promptly raced for third base. Fortunately, with me screaming from the third-base coach's box, he turned from his wayward way and safely reached first.)

So you get the idea: The (traditional) right-field fence was shallow, a mere 30 feet from home plate. The (traditional) left-field fence was 51 feet down the line, homers landing in Bendix Street and beyond.

Given such dimensions, you might assume that right-field was the poke of preference. But a mere five feet from the right-field fence was the garage of Mr. West, who spent nearly every waking hour working in that garage. Mr. West was a nice man; if he'd had a nickel for every Wiffle or tennis ball he tossed back in our yard during the nearly decade-long BBA existence, he could have bought the Yankees and had change to acquire Mike Piazza from the Mets.

But the BBA had a you-hit-it/you-get-it rule and nobody liked the hassle of climbing the fence and facing Mr. West. What further made right field a risky choice was that every obstacle around the field was live, meaning that a ball on Mr. West's slanted garage roof could, and sometimes would, bounce back into right field for an out.

Center field, 59 feet from the plate, was an all-but-impossible shot since a towering Douglas fir stood just beyond the pitcher's mound and not only took away dead center, but the power alleys as well. That, of course, meant (traditional) left field was homer heaven, which always rankled young Jared

McDonald, a left-handed hitter who had to go opposite field for his tators and still has about half a dozen would-be homers stuck in the bad-news branches of that tree.

Jesse, his younger brother, was a streak hitter, a kid whose first love was skateboarding and whose commitment to the game was forever being questioned by the press.

Jason, my younger, was the smallest of the four, the foul ball king. He would rip three or four foul balls into the rose bushes or onto our house's deck—we were continually restringing the wind chimes his great-grandfather, "Pop," made us—and then hit a double or triple down the line.

Ryan, my older, was the leader. He made the rules. ("If your team is ahead by 6, you have to bat opposite handed....No arguing....No changing rules during games, unless everyone agrees....")

He edited the *BBA News*, a computer-generated weekly. ("The Bendix Buddies team is without lead-off hitter Jesse McDonald because of contract complications....The second game of the doubleheader was cut short because it was past Jared's bedtime....The Bendix Buddies are having trouble keeping reporters out of the clubhouse....")

He drew up the contracts. ("I ＿＿＿ make a commitment to play on the Bendix Buddies baseball team. And to play to the best of my ability in every game. I promise to miss only ＿＿＿ practices and only ＿＿＿ games. If I happen to miss more of either I agree to be dealt a one-game suspension.")

He kept the statistics. ("Welch went 15-for-18 with four doubles, 14 RBIs, five home runs, and a grand slam, including two Effie Balls, one in the third deck.")

The ultimate hit was what the boys called an "Effie Ball," named in honor of Effie, the widow who lived across Bendix Street from the left-field fence, a woman who seemed to consider Wiffle balls in her rhododendrons more of an honor than an annoyance. Hitting Effie's duplex meant a blow of at least 100 feet, 120 to the second deck (the porch area above her garage) and 130 feet to the third and upper deck (her roof).

Games were usually two-on-two, often Ryan and Jared vs. the two younger boys. Sometimes, I was called to be "all-time pitcher" to both teams. On such occasions, I would, in the spirit of professional wrestling, create different personas for myself, including "Robo Pitcher," whose over-the-top jerky motion was always met with a barrage of boos, and the ever-controversial "Sidearm Sammy," a closer from the South who threw such a wicked sidearm pitch that he jokingly claimed he actually released the ball from a neighboring zip-code area.

Whatever moundsmen my mind could conceive, their common denominator was this: All got unmercifully shelled. You might say I had a multiple personality pitching disorder. I can still hear the hoots and hollers as I'd slink to the garden shed, i.e., "the shower," having once again been yanked by my impatient manager. And yet in the never-say-die spirit of sports, I would soon emerge—fist pumping in the air while the P.A. announcer introduced me—as some New Hope, the arm destined to bring this cocky kiddy corps to their humble knees.

Then one of the kids would do something like bounce a line drive off my forehead and it was back to the garden shed, the laughter from my opponents following me like pesky mosquitoes.

Like all good backyard leagues, what made BBA work was, as Yogi Berra might have said, 75 percent physical and the other half imagination. The boys would emerge from the house wearing the strangest uniforms imaginable—not some color-coordinated motif that came neatly folded in a box from Toys R Us, but wild stuff: multiple sweatbands, masking-taped numbers, batter's shin guards made from old football thigh pads, perhaps an ankle wrap to give them that "I'm-hurt-but-still-tough-enough-to-play" look.

We built a chicken-wire backstop and a plywood scoreboard—"Welch Stadium" it said—whose Home and Visitors numbers were changed by spinning four wooden dials about the sizes of large pizzas. The garden shed-turned-clubhouse was stocked with all sorts of bats—plastic, wood,

re-tooled broomsticks, duct-tape enhanced, you name it—
and other stuff: catcher's gear, Kool-Aid, cups, a chalkboard,
and a never-ending supply of sunflower seeds. Night games
were lit with a halogen floodlight positioned atop the shed.

We used mainly Wiffle balls until they inevitably cracked,
then we fortified them with duct tape, sometimes after wrap-
ping them in yarn so every ball wouldn't be an Effie Ball.

Videos were sometimes taken from a camera positioned
on our almost-flat back porch roof. A taped version of "The
Star-Spangled Banner" would begin special games,
including one World Series in which we invited Jared and
Jesse's parents over for grilled hot dogs and the game.

Occasionally, All-Star games would be played, an interesting concept since traditionally such games feature only
the league's best players, but I never remember any of the
four BBA players NOT making the team. I do remember
some suspensions, however; like life itself, BBA was not
without its darker side. As I recall, most suspensions
involved the younger two players not taking the game as
seriously as the older two thought necessary.

I remember a few thousand "out-safe" controversies—a
batter was out if he didn't reach second base before the ball was
thrown against the side of the house—and, of course, the controversial Deck Addition of '95, in which the Adult Housing
Authority allegedly ramrodded through a proposal to shave
off a smidge of the field as part of a kitchen add-on project.

"Smidge? You gotta be joking," said Ryan, the BBA's
union representative, whose defiance suggested the AHA's
proposal was like someone recommending taking off just a
smidge of Mona Lisa's smile.

The AHA won that battle and, in later years, was able to
put a small apple tree in foul territory down the (traditional)
first baseline. When BBA gave way in the mid-'90s to
teenagers with cars and jobs and arms so strong that Effie's
duplex would have been Wiffled to smithereens, a maple
tree went into shallow (traditional) right.

Like an Ebbets Field relic, the scoreboard now lies on the
side of the house, the victim of a decade of Oregon rain and

a designer who stupidly chose interior plywood. Last year, Effie moved to Idaho to be closer to her family. Ryan and Jared will be juniors in college this fall. Jesse spends more time driving a pickup than skateboarding.

The only one of the four BBA boys still playing organized baseball is my younger, Jason, the little kid in the Atlanta Braves hat who turned out to be the best of the bunch. Now 17, he made varsity as a sophomore, sometimes stepping to the plate and mentally cringing as someone in the crowd—that stupid guy who used interior plywood for the scoreboard—yells "BBA, baby" to remind him to relax and rip one down the line.

"Hello, Earth to Bob," said Sally, waking me from the past. "So, twenty-five cents for the hat?"

We sold a ton of stuff at the garage sale on that Saturday morning not long ago. We sold a refrigerator, exercycle, hundreds of golf balls, and a camp saw so cheaply made you'd have thought it came in a Cracker Jack box. We even sold a bunch of hats for a quarter apiece.

But Jason's Atlanta Braves hat never made it to the display floor. It now hangs proudly near my workbench, alongside one of his brother's. They are gentle reminders of the way it was on summer nights when little boys would slap a Wiffle ball into the sky and, their faces flushed with big-league determination and youthful innocence, race madly for third base.

Wings to Fly

Gayle's newsletter dated yesterday brought the glad tiding that you are blessed with an addition to the family. As time marches on, baby will need additional clothing, a catcher's mitt, baseball, or a bat. Realizing that these are all absolute necessities in the life of a boy, the enclosed check for $10 will help to supply them.

—Letter to my parents from my great grandfather
George Cook on the day after I was born in 1954.

Not long ago, I was driving through the downtown area of my old hometown when I saw it: a "Quitting Business" sign in front of Les & Bob's Sporting Goods. It hit me like walking through a cemetery and suddenly seeing a headstone of someone I hadn't known had died: At first, a touch of denial. This can't be; perhaps the store had just moved locations. Then, realizing otherwise, the inevitable questions: How? When? Why? And, finally, acceptance—and memories seemingly without end.

Memories not only about this particular place, but about this community of which the store had been a special part.

About the early '60s, a time so innocent that your biggest dilemma seemed to be getting tagged out while playing hot box with the Larkin brothers. About a boyhood spent on ball fields and in Friday-night gymnasiums that smelled of popcorn and on the cross-country trails of Avery Park.

I pulled over, walked back to the store, and peered through the dirty windows.

> The oil and leather smell of "The Claw," a baseball mitt I bought for $15 when I was 12...the sound of baseball cards in the spokes of my 24-inch Schwinn...the buzz of my Tudor Tru-Action electric football set, 22 red and yellow players jitterbugging in a vibrating frenzy, the ball carrier cradling the little felt "ball" and gloriously streaking down the sidelines—the wrong direction...

Les & Bob's was not where childhood dreams were born or played out. Instead, it was where dreams were given wings to fly—wings that came in size 3 Chuck Taylor Converse All-Star basketball shoes and Wilson "Ed-U-Cated" heel baseball gloves, and little silver needles through which air could inflate a flattened basketball, and a young boy's imagination.

In the 1960s, Les & Bob's was to the kids in my town what a general store in Springfield, Missouri, was to the people who came west on the wagon trains a century earlier—a place to get equipped for journeys to The Promised Land. Those journeys often turned out to be more promising in the minds of those taking them than in real life, which is perhaps why the place I got equipped still holds such fond memories: it was a place yet untarnished by life's inevitable defeats.

> The sound of a brand-new bat hitting a brand-new ball as I singled to center in the Midget League All-Star game...reading "Shorty at the State Tournament," the first sports book I can

remember...secretly listening to my transistor
radio in Mr. Brown's fourth-grade class at
Garfield School as Sandy Koufax and the Dodgers
beat the Yankees four straight in the '63 Series...

Unlike now, when you're not apt to find Mr. Good-
wrench checking your car's timing belt or Wendy cooking
your burger, when you walked into a sporting goods store
named Les & Bob's in 1965, chances were it was owned and
operated by a guy named Les and a guy named Bob. One of
them, Bob I think, wore lots of shaving lotion; he could be
helping a kid in the barbells section and you could smell
him from baseball bats. The two of them knew virtually
every kid who had ever played sports at Corvallis High
School; even if you were a so-so athlete like me, they made
you feel like an MVP. If you lived in Corvallis in the '50s and
'60s and bought a baseball glove or football pants or
catcher's mask, you bought it at Les & Bob's. Today, you can
get such items at just about any one-stop-shopping store in
Corvallis. And you can get way more than Les & Bob's
offered.

In the early '60s, the only type of sweatsuit you could
buy was the baggy gray kind. You couldn't buy sweatbands
because they hadn't been invented yet. Nor could you buy
the multitude of hats and shirts emblazoned with logos of
professional and college teams.

But even though, by today's standards, the choices at Les
& Bob's were limited, I never felt that way then. I felt like
when I walked into that store, anything was possible.

Playing hockey in Mark Baker's living room,
using his dad's putter and a three-iron for
sticks...building a scale model of Dodger Stadium
out of balsa wood...staying after Mr. Sprick's
social studies class at Cheldelin Junior High to
play "finger-kick football," in which we'd draw a
goalpost on the chalkboard, make these triangular
"footballs" out of notebook paper and, using the

flick of a finger, "kick" field goals. (Mr. Sprick, whose life in a wheelchair had left him with powerful arms and fingers, was our hero. He not only knew U.S. history, but could nail kicks from the back row with regularity.)

In the Les & Bob's sanctuary of sports, the ultimate chapel of dreams was a tiny nook in the back right corner: an area no larger than a small bedroom, lined floor to ceiling on three sides with shoes. It had a vinyl sofa, where you sat to be fitted.

To buy your first pair of Chuck Taylor Converse All-Star shoes at Les & Bob's was to engage in a rite of passage that seemed as hallowed as anything that might happen at church. The room had a smell like no other place: the smell of Chuck Taylor Converse All-Star rubber. The smell of newness. Of new seasons. Of beginnings.

You could buy a handful of specialty shoes at Les & Bob's—I still remember my royal blue Adidas Tokyo track shoes—but mainly what you could buy were Converse. And your choice of Converse was simple: black low-tops, black high-tops, white low-tops, and white high-tops.

When you laced up a pair of Chuck Taylor Converse All-Stars and realized they fit and your mother was standing nearby with the $8 to buy them, you felt you'd been given wings to fly. You felt like Billy Bam, the kid in the old Nestle's Quik commercials who, after gulping down a glass of chocolate milk, could play basketball at warp speed, scoring at will.

> Playing one-on-one football in front of Garfield School with Robbie Younger in the rain...CBS's star football announcer greeting his viewers with a nasally, "Hello, everybody, I'm Lindsey Nelson"... playing basketball on Sunday afternoons in Oregon State's Gill Coliseum, where Louisiana State's legendary "Pistol" Pete Maravich had once played a game, the only difference being Pete

didn't have to worry about a janitor kicking him
and his pals out ....

Near as I can tell, I made the first trip to Les & Bob's
when I was 8. I know this because I have, in an old scrapbook, the following letter, whose spelling and punctuation
I've left in their original state—the literary equivalent of a
box score forever preserved with embarrassing errors: "To
My Mom. I'm glad your my mother because your sweet and
kind and you let me go places like May 10th you took me to
Les & Bob's to get a baseball hat and you ironed the letters
OSU on it. I like you because your leting me go out for little
leaghg baseball. Love, Bobby."

> Listening to an Oregon State football game on the
> radio at my grandfather's beach cabin, Bob
> Blackburn's voice fading in and out, a thrilling
> touchdown run sometimes interrupted by a com-
> mercial for Ron Tonkin Chevrolet in Portland or a
> weather report from Salt Lake City or harumba
> music from Mexico...Mike Larkin showing me
> the old Bellfountain High basketball uniform that
> his father had worn in 1936 when the high school,
> which had two teachers and 29 students at the
> time, rose up to beat Franklin High of Portland in
> Oregon's version of "Hoosiers"...riding my
> bicycle five miles across town to Marysville Golf
> Course, my plaid bag of clubs on my shoulder....

In 1963, you could buy one style of kids' football pants at
Les & Bob's—cheesy red pants with cardboard thigh pads. I
wanted them desperately. If I got those pants, I figured, I
could someday be Heisman Trophy winner Terry Baker, the
Oregon State quarterback who, in 1962, won the Liberty
Bowl with a 99-yard touchdown run.

"Youre the best Mother in the world," I wrote my mother in
my grammar-impaired English, the rest of the sentence looking

like the remains of an Amtrak wreck. "Mother it is why you are going to buy that football sut with pads. thingk you."

> Playing an entire Far West Classic basketball tournament in my driveway with just me, an orange-covered scorebook I'd gotten for Christmas, and my imagination...the smell of the Willamette Valley's grass seed fields being burned in late August and realizing no matter how sickening the thought of school starting and me once again not getting the 64-crayon box like some other kids undoubtedly would get, all was well with the world because the smell of that smoke meant football was almost here...looking at the cleat marks in the mud of Spartan Field on foggy Saturday mornings, and thinking with awe that just the night before, I'd seen the very players who made those cleat marks.

I thought about Les & Bob's the other night when my wife and I were at a huge chain sporting good store in which one entire floor was devoted strictly to shoes. While waiting for my 17-year-old son to choose a pair of baseball shoes, I started counting the number of different styles available because I was amazed at the selection.

I counted three hundred and forty-seven different kinds. My wife and son thought I was crazy for counting the shoes; so, probably, did the clerk, a guy I'd never seen before and probably would never see again. But I was thinking about the little shoe room at Les & Bob's and how it probably had a dozen different styles at most, so I felt compelled to make the comparison.

My sons are growing up in a world so different from the one I did. Their high school football team plays its Friday night games on artificial turf at the University of Oregon, a couple of thousand spectators lost in a cavernous stadium, a place where players don't leave cleat marks for young boys to see the next morning. They laugh at my stories of Les &

Bob's shoe room, about plain gray sweatpants, about how few choices I had when I was growing up.

But, then, maybe that's what made my boyhood seem so strangely blessed, made the seemingly simple seem so profound, made what little we had seem so very, very big.

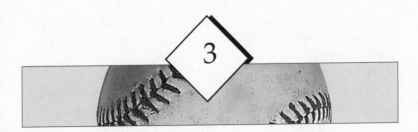

The Chosen One

On a December morning in 1969, dozens of sophomore boys at Corvallis High walked to the corner of the school gym and looked at a list posted on the wall. Those whose names were on the list were the Chosen Ones, 14 guys who would proudly don the powder blue and white Spartans uniforms to represent the school as its sophomore boys' basketball team.

Mine wasn't on it.

I scanned up and back, like the frantic mother in *The Deep End of the Ocean* looking for her kidnapped child in the hotel lobby—knowing, deep inside, my name wasn't there but figuring if I looked hard enough, it might somehow appear. But the little boy wasn't in that lobby and my name wasn't on that list.

When reality set in, there was only one thing to do: dabble in denial: There must be some mistake. Mr. Kinney, the varsity coach who had final say on all the teams, must have typed the alphabetical list the previous night and right after he'd typed Matt Wahl's name, he'd gotten distracted by something on "Rowan & Martin's Laugh-In." When he resumed his list-making, he hopped from Wahl to Yastrop, accidentally forgetting Welch. An innocent mistake; anyone could have made it.

Naw. There was no mistake.

When acceptance set in, there was only one thing to do: complain. Rail at the unfairness of life. Question the selections. One guy who made the team hadn't even been a starter on his junior high team as I had. Another couldn't fight his way out of a phone booth, much less get through a double screen.

But in the game of life, I'd been benched. Blame it on my 5-foot-6 height. With the exception of Mark Lasswell, a small guy who played with the intensity of a Chipmunk song, everyone on this team was roughly half a foot taller than me. In the last year, it was as if every kid my age had gotten on this bus whose marquee said "Puberty" and I was left back at the Greyhound station while some kind-hearted clerk said, "Don't worry, son. There'll be another bus by in a couple years. You can take it."

This wasn't fair. This was worse than the day during seventh-grade lunch when the going-steady ring I'd given Lowrey Beam came sliding down the cafeteria table, stopping near my fish sticks and Jell-O as if to mockingly say: *it's over, pal. You're history.*

As I walked down the hallway to my first-period class, that's how I felt. Like I was history. Like my athletic career was over at age 15. Like everyone in the hallway was looking at me and whispering: "Did you hear? He got cut."

But later that morning, something happened that would ultimately change everything. I was sitting in Mrs. Shaw's English class—I wonder if Hemingway ever got cut from his sophomore basketball team?—when a student office-worker politely interrupted the class to hand me a written message.

Normally, such messages spelled doom. Emergencies. Someone in your family had been in an accident or the principal had caught wind that it was you who, during the

Christmas concert, had paid Mark Baker the $20 to cluck like a chicken while doing a loop around the choir during "We Three Kings."

But I liked the timing on this one: Cuts posted this morning; message arrives an hour later. What I liked even better was the message itself: *See Coach Kinney ASAP.*

My sunken spirits rebounded. My imagination headed down court on a torrid fast break:

"...as I said, I'm sorry, Bob, I must have gotten distracted by something on 'Laugh-In'..."

Or maybe: "...and after thinking it over, I've decided to take 15 boys, not 14..."

Or perhaps: "...you've probably heard the tragic news about Mike Nelson having mononucleosis, meaning we need to replace him immediately..."

Suddenly, there I was, not surmising what Coach Kinney might say but actually sitting in the man's office, the office of the legendary varsity coach who had led Corvallis High to the state tournament with the regularity of spring itself.

"Bob," he said, "nobody hustled out there during try-outs more than you did."

Hallelujah! The man had come to his senses.

"You gave 110 percent at every practice."

So true, coach, but enough of this prelude; just tell me I'm going to be donning the Spartan powder blue and white. Just say it like this, coach: "Bob, how would you like to be on the sophomore basketball team?"

Coach Kinney ran a hand back through his crew cut and looked me dead in the eye.

"Bob," he said, "how would you like to be our junior varsity manager?"

It was as if someone suddenly pulled the plug on the jukebox of life. The music died. My world stopped spinning. My head tilted slightly forward in disbelief, my eyes unbelieving.

JV manager?

A pause ensued, the kind of perplexing pause that happens when life zigs when you expected it to zag.

What could I say? What I wanted to say was: Hold everything. Timeout, ref. What's going on here? Wrong call.

JV manager? This was like opening the largest, coolest-wrapped present under the Christmas tree and finding a rust-colored cardigan sweater knit by your grandmother, complete with outlines of the original 13 states on back.

JV manager? This was like wanting to be a movie director and instead selling popcorn and those industrial-sized boxes of Dots at the local twelve-plex.

"If you were a foot taller, you'd be out on that court yourself," the coach said, "but, Bob, every successful basketball team has a go-to guy, a manager who, well, is almost like a member of the team itself."

Right. Except while the players are running and gunning and having fun, this manager guy is keeping the shots-attempted chart and getting a sweat-top flung in his face.

"You'd be at every practice, travel with the team, eat meals with us, the works."

Gee, I've always wondered what it's like picking up towels in some exotic locker room like, say, the one at Sweet Home, built shortly after Lewis & Clark arrived in this neck of the woods.

"So what do you think, Bob? I think you'd make a great manager."

"Well, I, uh, was hoping"—the coach's eyes grew a tad larger and he slowly nodded his head in encouragement. "Uh, sure," I said. "I'll do it."

He stuck out his hand. "Great," he said. "Welcome to the team."

So I became the JV manager. I washed 12 basketballs before every practice. I rebounded for free-throw drills. I handed out uniforms. I made sure the water bottles were full. I kept statistics. I picked up towels.

Our coach was a man named Chris Christianson, a short man with a sardonic wit, elfin-like features, and a bow tie. He taught biology and seemed to think I was OK. We all called him Mr. Chris.

The players all called me "Bob." As in, "Bob, can I get a Band-Aid?" or, more formally, "Hey, Bob, what was my field goal percentage tonight?" But they seemed to like and respect me, partly because I knew a little bit about the game of basketball and partly because I was a sportswriter on the *High-O-Scope*, the student paper, and they knew I could blemish their young careers with a few clicks of my Smith-Corona.

Occasionally, I'd get in a pick-up game with some of the guys. I didn't want to be passing out towels for next year's JV team; I wanted to be the passee. I wanted to be proudly wearing the powder blue and white. So I needed to keep practicing.

The season began. All three teams—varsity, JV, and sophomore—started winning basketball games, and having fun in the process. Early in the season, the varsity blew out an opponent 117-61 and people started talking about how this was it—this was the year we might take state, something we'd never done before.

After the JVs would play, I got to watch every varsity game. Huge crowds packed each game—even on the road as opponents tried to stall the Spartan steamroller.

But nobody could. The varsity won 10 in a row, then stretched the streak to 15, 20, 21. Finally, it was the last regular game of the season for all three teams: the varsity was 21-0, the JVs 19-2 and the Sophomores 18-3.

Because we were playing our arch-rival Albany and a huge crowd was expected, the varsity and JV games were shifted to Oregon State University's Gill Coliseum. Everything was set for the crowning touch to our sensational season: playing the dastardly Albany Bulldogs in the final game on the same floor where some of the greatest collegiate players in the country, like UCLA's Kareem Abdul-Jabbar (then Lew Alcindor), had played.

One slight problem: at halftime, our JV team was down by 10 points to a team we had beaten easily earlier in the season. Except for the faint sound of the pep band, the locker room was dead quiet as the 14 players sat on the benches. Mr. Chris stared at the floor. I stood off to the side, towel in hand.

Mr. Chris had a temper, and I had a feeling the teapot was about to blow. Sure enough, he launched into a red-faced tirade, the kind of speech he must have heard a hundred times back in boot camp. He paused to mentally reload.

"You know what bothers me most? You guys don't even care! You act like you don't even wanna be out there! Like you're too worried about who you're taking to the dance tomorrow night! Like you don't even care about the game of basketball! Well let me tell you, it's a privilege to play basketball! A privilege!"

Another pause. He had softened 'em up with an aerial attack. Now he was going to bring in the ground troops. He was going to say something inspirational. He was going to say something that reached to the core of their souls. He was going to say—

"You see that kid over there?" the coach said, not in my mind but to everyone in that locker room.

Huh? He pointed to me. Fourteen heads turned my way.

"Gentlemen," he said slowly, "I've got a manager who would give his left testicle to be out there on that floor in Spartan blue, playing the game that you don't seem to give a rip about."

Another pause.

"Think about it."

Believe me, I was. I wanted to say, "Who, me?" I wanted to say, "Uh, coach, it's true that I love the game, but...." I wanted to say, "I know you mean well, Mr. Chris, but next time you might wanna clear some of your motivational examples with me before...."

But Coach Kinney, the man who had hired me for this hallowed position, had been right. I wasn't just the manager. I was, well, like a member of the team. So I just pursed my lips a bit and nodded my head slowly, as if to say: "Yep, fellas, Coach is right. So whataya gonna do about it?"

What they did about it was go out and absolutely thrash Albany in front of the largest crowd that had ever seen a JV basketball game in the history of Corvallis High. It was among the most amazing displays of Jekyll-and-Hyde athleticism I would see in decades of watching sports, a comeback for the ages.

The varsity went on to win all its games to become the first team in the state of Oregon to go undefeated en route to the Class AAA championship: twenty-six wins, no losses. After the championship game, fans drove the two hours from Portland to Corvallis where the parents of one of our star players opened their ice cream shop up at midnight to celebrate.

There had never been a varsity basketball season like that one in the history of our school, nor has there been one since. And I saw every one of those victories. Rode on the same bus with those guys. And, of course, became the George Gipp of JV halftime talks, the star of a story that still gets told at an occasional high school reunion, along with the football story about linebacker Ken Maddox accidentally intercepting a pass when a hard-thrown ball wedged between his facemask and helmet.

But there's more:

In a world big on getting, I learned how to give a little more that winter. In a world big on power, I learned how to serve a little more. In a world big on pride, I learned how to humble myself a little more. At the time, I can't say I noticed such profundity in my midst, but life's lessons sometimes bear fruit well after the season in which they are planted.

I never did wear the powder blue and white of a Spartan basketball uniform. Nor did I hand out another towel. I didn't even make the yearbook photo as JV manager, having been sick the day the photographer came. But I'll always remember the winter of 1969-70 as a time when I learned that, even when your name isn't on the list, life goes on.

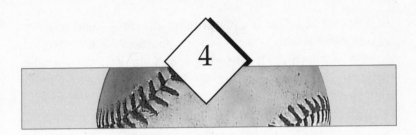

Trading Places

Every now and then I think back to something in my past and say to myself: Did I really do that? It's not as if my past could create a 10-part miniseries on boyhood evil, but just the same, directors would be hard-pressed to fit it all in a two-hour docudrama.

One incident, in particular, has dogged me over the years—31 years, to be exact. An incident in which my motives seemed innocent enough at the time and yet triggered something tragic.

It was the fall of 1968 and I was a reserve halfback for the Cheldelin Junior High football team. As time slipped by, I would remember three things about that season.

First, that we got to practice on grass instead of sawdust. The school was in only its second year and the previous season, because our grass hadn't yet been planted, we'd practiced in sawdust for three months. And itched for three months. And heard our mothers complain about sawdust in their washing machines for three months.

Second, that I scored an extra point—my only score ever in organized tackle football—in our stunning 19-6 upset of

Western View. I was a second-team running back and my scrapbook statistics—kept in a manila folder labeled "Memories"—show I carried the ball three times for five yards, an impressive 1.67-yards-per-carry average. I played so little that, along with fellow scrub Cortney Burris, I would rub mud on my thigh pads so when the game was over, our fans—particularly the young female fans—might think I'd actually seen action. But against Western View, in a game in which our star halfback, John Spain, had mowed down defenders like a runaway tank, I was thrown in at the end of the game, given a hand-off, and somehow scored, a feat which seems all the more remarkable considering I think I ran those three yards with my eyes closed.

And finally, I remember that I did something I've always regretted. It came during a routine drill called the meat grinder. It was simple: There were two lines, offense and defense, runners and tacklers. A runner was tossed the ball and a kid from the other line came up and tackled him. One on one. Pride vs. pride—all of it done in front of a couple of coaches and about two dozen teammates, hootin' and hollerin'.

As I waited my turn in the running back line, I did what any self-respecting 110-pound halfback concerned about his immediate future would do: I counted ahead to see what defensive player I would draw. John Spain. (Cue "Dragnet" theme song.)

Perhaps I'd miscounted. Please, Lord, may I have miscounted. Nope. A recount showed I was the seventh offensive player and he was the seventh defensive player. John Spain was a guy who had been shaving since he was roughly 9. A guy who'd been held back a year and, thus, was a year older than the rest of us, maybe a couple. A guy with Popeye arms and fire-hydrant thighs—and yet was so fast that Oregon State's track coach was already eyeing him for the 100-yard dash. A guy who, well, could be mean.

John had jet black hair, piercing eyes, and stubble by noon. Off the field, he was Mr. Mellow; we were casual friends and had metal shop together. But on the field, he had this sort of hypnotic look in his eyes, like a mad truck driver wanting to make Atlanta in time for WWF wrestling on a motel TV.

What frightened me wasn't so much that he outweighed me by a good 75 pounds and was 5-foot-10 to my 4-foot-11. What frightened me was remembering the time he hit another scrub, Todd Cirilli, so hard that Todd's helmet popped off like a champagne cork.

Sizing up the situation, I did what any self-respecting conniver would do: I turned to the running back behind me, Ricky Root, and casually asked if he would like to trade places. In retrospect, it was like a passenger on the Titanic politely asking to borrow a life jacket from a passenger who hadn't heard the news yet.

Like me, Ricky Root was a second- or third-stringer. Unlike me, though, he wasn't the kind of wimp who would actually count ahead to see what defender he might be facing in the meat grinder drill. Nor was he the kind of guy who would stop to wonder why I might be asking that sort of question. I don't remember much about him, other than that he had gone to Mountain View grade school, which is one of the district's poorer, rural schools. For some reason, I sensed he'd had a pretty tough upbringing.

"Trade places?" he asked.

"Yeah," I said.

"Sure," he said. "Why not?"

For a few moments, I felt a little like I imagine Houdini felt when he had once again cheated death. There I had been, handcuffed inside the chain-secured coffin, 60 feet beneath the East River in freezing temperatures and, suddenly, I was on the surface, alive!

"Root vs. Spain," yelled Coach Osborne. His whistle blew. John Spain bolted forward like a rodeo bull uncaged.

Ricky Root faked right, faked left, and then was torpedoed onto his back.

Thud. The hit had a sickening sound to it, like a 50-pound sack of sugar being dropped from a second-story roof. But the sound of the hit was quickly replaced by the sound of Ricky Root's half-moan, half-scream.

The football had popped loose, though nobody bothered to retrieve it. Players in both lines stood wide-eyed, waiting to assess the carnage. John Spain got up off the ground. Ricky Root did not.

Instead, he lay there on his back, writhing in pain. One of his legs was pinned back in a discombobulated position, like that of a rag doll tossed from the top of a bunk bed.

"Quick," somebody said, "call an ambulance."

When it arrived, it drove right onto the practice field. The EMTs took off Ricky's helmet and carefully placed him on a stretcher. And just like that, he was gone.

I never played organized football after that year; neither, to my knowledge, did Ricky Root. He never said anything to me about the incident, nor I to him. I saw him on and off in high school. He was what we called a "hard guy," a "parking lot" guy. He wore a leather jacket and smoked. His photo never appeared in my three annuals; his name wasn't among the Class of '72 graduates. He never made it to any class reunions.

From time to time, I wonder what happened to Ricky Root—and if the meat grinder incident made what may have been a tough life for him even tougher. From time to time, I think we all look back with regret at things we did or didn't do, incidents in which we never intended for someone to get hurt but they did anyway.

One day, I checked a Corvallis phone book to see if he still lived in town. Nope. I went to the public library and did a computer search for all the Rick, Richard, and Ricky Roots in the United States, and came up with 24, including two Richards in Oregon. I was thinking that even though the incident happened three decades ago, I might call and tell him what a selfish jerk I'd been. Say I'm sorry.

I didn't make that call. But when I went to throw out the page with the phone numbers on it, instead I created a file—"Root, Ricky"—and stowed the list away, just in case I ever find the courage that I somehow think I should.

Rental Clubs

I could barely hear the voice on the other end of the long-distance call. "Dad," said my 19-year-old son Ryan, "I just played the worst two rounds of golf since I was a sophomore in high school."

Along with his college golf team, he had entered this out-of-state tournament with great expectations. With just a single round left to play, he now had no expectations. He was so disappointed he could barely talk, much less motivate himself to bounce back.

He was the two-time champion of our city's only 18-hole public course. As a freshman, he shot a final-round 69 to win the conference's fall championship. But on this rainy April day, 18 months later, he had shot 94 and 93, scores usually reserved for guys like me.

"I am one bad golfer," he said.

"Ry, you're a great golfer who had one bad day," I said.

What made it worse was that his cousin Brad, who lived nearby but had never seen him play, had followed him around.

"I'm so embarrassed," Ryan said.

Perhaps you know what it's like to be a parent in a situation like this. You want to say something profound, something emotionally invigorating, something that will instill hope in a child of yours who has none. But the more you talk, the more you realize how uninspiring you are. The "tomorrow-will-be-another-day" stuff doesn't cut it with a kid who has just made more double bogeys in a day than he usually makes in a season.

Still, sometimes when we open the refrigerator of our minds, all we find is leftovers. I reached behind the mayonnaise for the two-day-old pizza wrapped in aluminum foil.

"Hey," I said. "Tomorrow's another day. Forget what happened today. Go out there, remember who you are, remember what you've done in the past, and have fun."

I heard this slight half groan on the other end of the line, like someone waking up after gallbladder surgery.

"I'll be praying for you, buddy," I said.

For Ryan, the next day dawned a lot like the previous day: rainy. The coach drove the team from the motel to the course. Ryan was standing outside the van, talking with his cousin-the-masochist—back for the final round despite having seen the first two—and turned to get his clubs.

That's when he noticed his coach was driving out of the club's parking lot—with Ryan's clubs still inside the van. All the other players had gotten theirs except for him. Ryan figured the coach was just going to get a quick cup of coffee. But about 45 minutes before his tee time, Ryan asked a teammate where the coach had gone.

"To a tire shop to get the spare fixed."

Gulp.

Ryan's cousin had a car. The two of them jumped in and started frantically scouring the streets of Olympia, Washington, looking for a white van on a garage hoist. No luck. They stopped and asked directions to the nearest tire shop and found it, but the coach wasn't there. They headed back to the golf course. No van. No coach. No clubs.

"Next up on the tee," said a voice on the loudspeaker, "the threesome of Ryan Welch of Linfield College..."

Tournament golf, you may know, is a game of precise rules, one of which says that if you aren't able to hit your ball when it's your turn to tee off, you're toast. DQ'd. Disqualified.

Instincts kicked in. Ryan raced into the pro shop and spewed his dilemma. A pro shop attendant responded like a good EMT, throwing together a bag of rental clubs to stabilize this young man's life until the ambulance—a white van with a set of golf clubs inside—could arrive on the scene.

At one point, the bag had a left-handed seven-iron in it; Ryan isn't left-handed. The final concoction looked like this: 10 clubs (you're allowed 14), including a crooked putter and a demo driver that, says Ryan, "was like swinging a shovel."

A teammate handed him a handful of well-beaten balls. Despite slick conditions, he was forced to wear a pair of running shoes, not golf spikes.

It wasn't a pretty start. He double bogeyed the first two holes, a pace that had him on target for 108, and set up the kind of moment that, in our family, reminds us all of the scene in the movie *Trading Places* when Dan Akroyd—a once-wealthy man who had the world at his fingertips—finds himself standing on the sidewalk in the rain, dressed as Santa Claus, his beard matted with fried chicken. What, he wonders, could possibly be worse than this?

Slowly, Akroyd looks down and sees what could be worse than this: a dog has mistaken his leg for a fire hydrant.

But no dog came sniffing Ry's golf shoes on this soggy morning. Instead, on the third hole, he rolled in a 12-foot birdie—his first of the tournament. On the fifth hole, he drained a 50-foot birdie.

He suddenly had new hope, a new attitude, and a red-hot rental putter.

He continued to play solid, and sometimes spectacular, golf. On the 18th hole, after scuffing the shovel driver 75 yards off the tee, he scrambled to within 8 feet of the hole, sank a putt and posted a 79. He had played the final 16 holes in just three over par, posted the best score on the team, and finished among the top 10 for the day.

❖   ❖   ❖

I often tell this story at men's retreats because I believe it says something about life and circumstances and how we react to those circumstances. On my wall hangs a tattered quote from Chuck Swindoll:

> We cannot change our past. We cannot change the fact that people will act in a certain way. We cannot change the inevitable. The only thing we can do is play on the one string we have, and that is our attitude. I am convinced that life is 10 percent what happens to me and 90 percent how I react to it.

Ryan didn't get to choose what clubs he played with on this particular day. But he did have a say in how he was going to respond to that situation. Low as he was, he somehow mustered what little hope he had to not only weather the storm, but to rise above it.

Beyond the golf course, life sometimes swirls with much stiffer challenges. Ryan's cousin, Brad, who tromped 54 holes with his pal in the rain and mud over those two days, couldn't stop his younger brother from falling into an icy river and dying on the last day of 1994. But he did have a say in how he was going to respond to that tragedy, and he courageously chose to not give up on life or God or himself in the years that followed.

A young man at a men's retreat I was leading couldn't stop his father from committing suicide when the boy was only 5 years old. But he did have a say in how he was going to respond to that tragedy—and now is a committed father, husband, and servant of God who is intent on starting a new legacy for his own son.

After I told the story of Ryan's golf comeback, I asked the men at that retreat if anyone could relate with their own lives—lives whose obstacles were far more treacherous than sand traps and split-level greens.

Men are often reluctant to share from their hearts, but the man whose father had killed himself stood up and began his story with a line I will never forget.

"You might say life gave me the rental clubs," he said.

But the triumph of his testimony—and of all those who rise above the circumstances—is in an attitude that says the strength inside me can overcome whatever's outside me.

It's an attitude that says I'll trust God even when I don't understand why my clubs weren't there for me.

It's not looking back, not even ahead, but looking up— "from whence my strength cometh," says Isaiah.

It's playing those rental clubs for all they're worth, which is a lot when in the hands of a faithful follower.

Ashes and Dust

Jennie, Jennie, you've got to understand. I believe that God made me for a purpose. For China. But He also made me fast, and when I run I feel his pleasure. To give it up would be to hold Him in contempt.

—Eric Liddell in *Chariots of Fire*

When seeing me run cross-country in high school, I'm not sure if God felt pleasure or if He just winced; I was no Eric Liddell, a gold medal winner in the 1924 Olympics who went on to become a missionary in China. But my days as a competitive runner taught me life lessons that I still lean on three decades later: To push myself to the limits. To endure even when it hurts and I'm far behind the leaders. And to only run in Doberman-free zones.

I fell in love with running accidentally on purpose. The accidental part was that when I turned out for eighth-grade track, the coaches relegated me to the 1320 (three-lap) event because I was too slow, weak, and un-springy for anything else. The on-purpose part was that, as a ninth-grader, I saw

All-American runner Steve Prefontaine of Coos Bay, Oregon, set a national two-mile record on the very Corvallis High track on which I would train the next fall if I ran cross-country.

So I turned out for the team. Not because, like the lame man touching the robe of Jesus, I thought running on the same track as "Pre" would miraculously heal me of my distance-running deficiencies. But because watching Prefontaine run awakened something deep inside me: I was drawn by the simplicity of a sport that was basically man vs. time. I was drawn by the proverbial loneliness of the long-distance runner; you either succeeded or failed all on your own. And I was drawn by the realization that for a 125-pound kid who would rather eat raw brussels sprouts for a week than wrestle, running was my last best hope to stay involved in sports.

Unlike Prefontaine, I did not set my sights on a national record. My goal was much less lofty: to someday run in the Oregon State Class AAA cross-country meet. Pre had won the event as a junior and senior; I just wanted to be invited to the party. It became my quiet crusade.

I could qualify for the state cross-country race in one of two ways: by finishing as one of the top seven individuals in the district meet or by being on one of the top two teams. I ran JV as a sophomore. I didn't make it as a junior on varsity; neither did the team. Thus, I had one last chance to make state—my senior year.

Because of teammates graduating, moving, and suffering collapsed lungs because of overzealous trumpet blowing, I suddenly found myself going into the summer before that year as Corvallis High's top runner. It was like one of those disaster movies in which, after the plane crashes, the entire flight crew dies and some nerd gets appointed leader because he once earned a Cub Scouts Wolf Badge for successfully making bread-on-a-stick.

But I had three months to prepare for the start of the season, and I vowed to simply be the best runner I could be. My opening workout, May 24, 1971, wasn't particularly promising:

> *Jog 440. 3-mile all out in 19:02. Muscles didn't hurt.*
> *Stomach did. Barfed. Jog 3/4 mile.*

June 3rd's entry wasn't much more encouraging:

> *Ran 3 miles to Skyline West before a dog bit me and I*
> *got lost. Disappointing workout. I'll bounce back.*

And I did. After summer days of raking green beans onto a conveyor belt at a cannery, I would ride my bicycle three miles home, change into my running gear, and be off.

Almost always by myself, I ran the country roads around Corvallis, into McDonald Forest, to the top of Ivy Hill. I ran carefully selected routes that took me by the houses of girls who, I always hoped, would be gazing out their windows, awaiting their knight in Property of CHS armor. (No such luck.) I ran to Oregon State's track and did timed laps. I ran stadium stairs. On family vacations, I ran at the beach and on hiking trails high in the Cascade Mountains. I ran all-comers meets every few weeks to test myself.

Each workout became a test, a challenge, a step that would reward me in the cool of autumn, when I'd be trying to pass some South Salem runner in Avery Park. As I pounded my way up Norwood Hill and headed for the telephone-pole finish line in front of my house, I'd imagine it to be the final 100 yards of the district cross-country race.

I'd glance at my hand-held stopwatch and if it read, say, 57:17, I'd pretend that I had to beat 57:30 to finish seventh and make it to state. Then, just like Pre, I'd kick into over-drive, as a small crowd—say, Mrs. Rudinsky, raking her lawn, and my dad, sanding a boat in our driveway—turned and looked. Chest burning and knees pumping, I headed for the finish line.

I charted every workout on the backs of order forms used by my father's photography business. I meticulously kept track of every mile run—639 1/2 as a junior and 744 as a senior, a combined amount, I later figured, that would get me from Seattle to L.A. I also rated each workout, four dots for an outstanding effort and one dot for poor.

For example, I gave myself one dot for this workout on August 9:

> *I feel a little guilty about not running my long workout tonight, but not all that guilty. I was going to run Sunday night until this trip to Triangle Lake came up. I want to be a good, solid runner that people can look at and say, "There's a runner," but I simply am not willing to let running rule my life. By the way, the water skiing was great.*

I gave myself four dots for a workout on July 17— because I ran a marathon. These were the days before marathons meant 10,000 people oozing across the Brooklyn Bridge in New York City. Before people realized that it might not be a smart idea to hold a 26-mile race in the dead of summer, particularly one starting as late as 9 A.M. on an 85-degree day, as this one did.

After running for 22 miles, getting a drink at a farmhouse, walking three miles, then plodding the final mile, I crossed the finish line. I remember seeing the end of the 1968 Olympics marathon in Mexico City on TV, the runners triumphantly entering the stadium to the cheers of 80,000 people. When I arrived at Newberg High—photos don't lie—exactly seven people were on hand: three other runners, three meet officials, and a former Corvallis runner named Ted Wolfe, who was my ride home.

A young woman behind a card table handed me a certificate that said "Berrian Festival marathon 1971"—yep, marathon was misspelled. I finished in four hours, 19 minutes and 25.4 seconds. But that was good enough for tenth place! That night, I wrote in my journal: "I must admit, I'm inspired."

While raking beans each day at the cannery, I daydreamed about the state cross-country meet and, more immediately, about breaking five minutes in the mile. I had broken 5:10 half a dozen times, even run 5:00.0, but never been officially below the Bannister-plus-a-minute barrier. Later that summer, I did it in an all-comers meet.

> *This may sound stupid a long time from now, but I'm happy. 4:59.8: I won! I like the feeling of winning.*

I had once won a 440-yard race at an all-comers meet because the only other runner was a shot-putter trying to get in shape for football. But my win in the mile was the first time I'd ever won a distance race of any sort.

It would also be my last.

August 17:

> *If tonight wasn't a near-exhaustive workout, I'm not Pre Welch. 22 miles. Last hill was a killer. My eyes are hardly staying open. I'm sick. Thanks for letting me make it home, God.*

Two days later I ran a steeplechase race and an all-out 440 at an all-comers race. "Leg sore," I reported in the journal. The next day I ran 16 miles.

Cross-country practice began August 31. On September 1, my journal reported that despite the sore leg, I ran five miles by myself in the morning, then 11 x 220s and 4 x 440s during the team's workout.

> *I took off and went fairly hard, feeling great. Left everyone behind. I really like being the leader, the best. I'm going to work my tail off this fall. I'm really happy.*

September 9:

> *Leg hurting real bad. Pain on front bone and almost everywhere in the middle.*

September 10:

> *Tried running but simply couldn't.*

September 20:

> *Saw the doctor. Told me I tore a muscle and to stay off for two weeks.*

I had shin splints in one of my legs. I'd overrun. Too many miles. Too little rest. My season, the doctor said, was probably over. It couldn't be over, I told him; I was a senior. I needed to run at district so I could qualify for state.

My coach put me on a swimming and weight lifting program with hopes that I might be ready to run one dual meet, then district. On October 14, I toed the line for my first competitive race in more than a month. I had trained little, but somehow felt that I could run strong. I was wrong. I finished 17th out of 17.

But my journal suggested I wasn't quitting.

> *Oddly enough, I'm confident for district. I'm just going to make up my mind and go when it hurts. I'm going to kill myself but I'm going to run well.*

My state-meet dream died in a driving rainstorm. I finished 34th, 27 places behind what I needed to qualify for state. The team finished third. Nobody from Corvallis High was going to state. The season was over. My high school career was over.

Afterward, I thought back to those hot summer nights, chugging up Norwood Hill to finish yet another workout, buoyed by whatever challenge I'd made for myself and met.

Now I sat in a cold bus, raindrops slaloming down the windows, teammates filing past me and, I supposed, thinking that I'd failed them, the school, perhaps all of Western Civilization.

I've thought a lot about that season in the years since: how hard I had worked and how, in the end, all those miles and side aches—all that sweat and sacrifice—seemed to be for naught, a season summed up in a silly graph I created on a sheet of notebook paper: "How Shin Splints Affected Me," my miles-per-week looking so impressive, then plummeting like the Crash of '29.

What I've realized is that the experience was all for naught only if I believe value is limited to outcome, not process. It was for naught only if I believe value is limited to what the world allows us to qualify for—be it a record, a medal, or an invitation to a state cross-country meet, and not God's deeper purpose. It was for naught only if I failed to realize that some of life's best lessons are learned not through achieving, but in simply trying.

God didn't make me fast, like Liddell and Pre, but He did make me for a purpose, and I'm convinced that every mile I ran that summer had meaning to it. Every mile meant something beyond a scrawled line in my journal. Every mile was some sort of piece in the puzzle of who I would eventually become and how I would react when life as an adult got painful and when I realized I was far behind the leaders and when I simply wanted to quit, but did not.

Author Jack London, whose stories often examined man's courage to survive in a Yukon environment much harsher than a small-town high school's, once wrote:

> I would rather be ashes than dust! I would rather that spark should burn out in a brilliant blaze than it should be stilled by dry rot....The proper function of man is to live, not to exist. I shall not waste my days trying to prolong them. I shall use my time.

Man vs. time. Nearly 30 years have passed since those summer evenings when I'd pound up Norwood Hill, and I'm still running. A few years back, I ran another marathon, at 41. I've run in the largest running-relay in the world, the Hood to Coast. I've run in the deep heat of the South, in the deep snows of Central Oregon. I've run along Canada's Lake Ontario, at dawn high above the Grand Canyon, on rutted roads in Haiti with a dozen barefoot children glee-fully following my every step. Don't get me wrong; I'm still a hack. But I still run.

Just a few days ago, I was finishing an early-morning run on an Oregon beach when, just before Starr Creek, about 200 yards from the rocks I call my finish line, I glanced at my digital wristwatch: 49:19.

Instinctively, I kicked into overdrive. I splashed through the creek, a couple of curious beachcombers looking up from their shell-searching to watch. What they saw, I suppose, was mid-life madness. What I saw was something else: the finish line of a cross-country course. And if I could break 50 minutes, a chance to finish seventh, and make it to state.

The Revolutionary

I remember it in the same way I remember watching the grainy footage of Neil Armstrong walking on the moon: with a sense of awe and wonder that the unreachable dream had been reached. But as I watched ABC's coverage of the high-jump event in the 1968 Olympic Games in Mexico City, what made the moment so meaningful was that I felt a personal connection to an athlete who, with one small leap, would change sports history forever.

When U.S. high jumper Dick Fosbury sprinted, sprang, arched his back, and cleared the bar at 7 feet 4 1/4 inches to win the Olympic gold medal, he revolutionized the event; his victory validated a new, unorthodox style of jumping that until then had been seen as little more than Foz's Folly. He literally turned his back on The Establishment—and had the last laugh.

What's more, his triumph made a statement about daring to be different. About the power of thinking beyond the lines. About the limitations of doing things a certain way only because "we've always done it this way."

And what personalized it all for me was that Fosbury had perfected his craft virtually in my backyard, on foam rubber pads at Oregon State University's Bell Field—where my buddies and I would flop ourselves come Sunday afternoons. He was our hero. He was our inspiration. And we honored him by giving up the old—the conventional "western roll"—and embracing the new: the Fosbury Flop.

❖ ❖ ❖

Jesus was a revolutionary. He turned his back on The Establishment. He dared to be different. He thought, spoke, and acted outside the lines. He never did anything simply because that's the way it had always been done.

He dared to push the cultural limits. He refused to live within the Phariseeical box that the church leaders had established. He not only had the vision to see beyond the self-imposed limitations of man, but the courage to venture beyond.

By the Sea of Galilee, he climbed the side of a mountain, turned to the multitudes and said: "You have heard that it was said, 'Love your neighbor and hate your enemy.' But I tell you: Love your enemies and pray for those who persecute you, that you may be sons of your Father in heaven. He causes His sun to rise on the evil and the good, and sends rain on the righteous and the unrighteous. If you love those who love you, what reward will you get? Are not even the tax collectors doing that? And if you greet only your brothers, what are you doing more than others? Do not even the pagans do that?" (Matthew 5:43-47).

In short, he boldly raised the bar.

❖ ❖ ❖

The Fosbury Flop high jump style was born in near-obscurity in 1963 on a high school field in Medford, Oregon, then a town of 29,000, in southern Oregon. A gangly kid, Fosbury had begun high-jumping at the age of 11, using what was called the scissors method, a stand-up style popularized by children leaping small fences while being chased by large dogs.

He wasn't very good. His coach encouraged him to learn the traditional western roll, in which the jumper approached at an angle, flung one foot up and over the bar, then did a sort of sideways roll with the rest of the body. He was even worse using that method. "Dick wasn't a prospect," his old high school coach joked, "He was a suspect."

As a sophomore, Fosbury scissored his way to 5-feet-4 inches and suddenly got an idea. "I began to feel what I needed to do was raise my hips so I wouldn't be knocking the bar off with my rear end. And when I raised my hips, I began to drop my shoulders and lay back."

The result looked chaotic, as if two shot-putters had grabbed him by the arms and legs and flung him over the bar backwards. But it worked. Fosbury cleared 5-foot-10 and qualified for the district meet. It was a total shock to everyone, including himself.

As he perfected the style, first at Medford High and later at Oregon State, the shockwaves got broader. But so did the bad-mouthing. A fellow OSU jumper took one look at his style and laughed.

"To be honest," he said later, "I thought his style was a joke."

But when Fosbury set an OSU record by leaping 6-10 as a sophomore, nobody was laughing anymore. The next year he cleared the seven-foot barrier to win an indoor meet in Oakland, California, and made the cover of *Track & Field News*. In the photo, skeptical straddlers, arms folded, watched this new-fangled flop. Remembers a fellow OSU jumper: "It was like in *Butch Cassidy and the Sundance Kid* when Butch says, 'Who are those guys?' Only this time it was, 'Who is this guy?' "

The King of the Universe was born not in a palace, but in obscurity—a stable in Bethlehem, a small town in the land of

Judah. When he was 12, he attended a Feast of the Passover, got separated from his parents, and was later found in the temple courts, sitting among the teachers, listening to them, and asking them questions.

He grew in wisdom and stature and dared to confront the Pharisees, kings of conventional thinking. They wallowed in self-righteousness. They hid behind hard-and-fast laws built on tradition but lacking in heart. If someone were drowning in a water hole posted with a No Swimming sign, they would piously obey.

"I tell you the truth," Jesus said to them, "the tax collectors and the prostitutes are entering the kingdom of God ahead of you" (Matthew 21:31).

Skeptical, the Pharisees stood by, arms folded. They looked at Jesus as a suspect. To them, this new agenda looked chaotic, as if he had no respect for the tried-and-true ways of tradition. They mocked him. They tried to trip him up.

One of them tested him with this question: "Teacher, which is the greatest commandment in the Law?" Jesus replied: " 'Love the Lord your God with all your heart and with all your soul and with all your mind'. This is the first and greatest commandment. And the second is like it: 'Love your neighbor as yourself' " (Matthew 22:36-39).

Love? Relationships? The skeptical Pharisees, arms folded, watched this newcomer. *Who is this guy?*

❖ ❖ ❖

In Corvallis, they started calling Fosbury "The Wizard of Foz." High-jumping was hot. My friends and I—14 at the time—made weekly pilgrimages to Bell Field, which was usually open and would sometimes have a foam pit, standards, and crossbar available for use. Once, while I was home sick, my mother left to run some errands and I propped a piece of 8-foot molding across two adjustable music stands. My bed made a fine landing pit. Though I could only manage a three-step approach, I won an Olympic gold medal that morning—despite a nagging cold.

Fosbury, meanwhile, went from being ranked in a 13-way tie for 48th in the world to the champion of the world—in less than a year. In the 20 years following his gold-medal leap, 18 of 24 Olympic medalists used the Fosbury Flop; the last time a non-Flopper even placed in the men's competition was 1972.

Fosbury's career, in essence, ended that day. But the revolution had begun.

In Jerusalem, they started calling Jesus the Messiah. He went from an unknown carpenter to the most controversial figure in the history of time. He turned water into wine. He healed the sick. Made the blind to see, the lame to walk. He broke the cultural taboos and struck up a conversation with a Samaritan woman at a well, and, instead of railing about her adultery, told her about something better: Living Water. Spiritual Salve. Himself.

He told people to treat others like they'd want to be treated themselves.

He told people to stop worrying; God would take care of them. "See how the lilies of the field grow. They do not labor or spin. Yet I tell you that not even Solomon in all his splendor was dressed like one of these. If that is how God clothes the grass of the field which is here today and tomorrow is thrown in the fire, will he not much more clothe you, O you of little faith?" (Matthew 6:28-30).

He told people if they wanted rest, to come unto him. If they were looking for answers, he had them. "Ask and it will be given to you. Seek and you will find."

He wept at a friend's death. And kept saying stuff that comforted the afflicted and afflicted the comfortable.

When the Pharisees ganged up on a woman caught in adultery, he told her to quit sinning, but refused to condemn her. And forgave her. "If any one of you is without sin," he told the Pharisees, "let him be the first to throw a stone at her."

He called the Pharisees a "brood of vipers." He told them to remove the speck in their own eye before trying to remove the log in someone else's. To quit saying how righteous they were and, instead, be like the tax collector who said, "God, have mercy on me, a sinner."

Pretty soon, they'd had enough. They had Jesus arrested, even though the governor himself asked, "What crime has he committed?" They had him killed. But three days later, the earth shook, and the tomb was empty.

The revolution had begun.

The Coach

❖ ❖ ❖

Coaches are the first to arrive. They make sure the equipment is there. They choose the team, run the drills, and fire up the players. They encourage, remind, instruct, and, sometimes, explode. They're the last to leave. And the first to arrive again, as the cycle begins anew.

First Season

In every coach's memory, there lives a first season. Mine unfolded when I was 23 years old. I can't remember why I agreed to coach baseball—temporary insanity comes to mind—but I was handed a rag-tag group of fifth-graders formed by taking the stragglers from the league's six other teams. It was like trying to decorate your living room with garage-sale items that hadn't sold by noon.

The only thing we had less of than talent was confidence. "Coach," said one boy while warming up at our first practice, "I think we're going to lose a lot this year."

"But how can you say that?" I said. "You haven't even seen the other players yet. We're an expansion team, sure, but we might be good."

"It's just a feeling I have," he said.

The kid turned out to be a good hitter and a good fielder. But his greatest gift, I soon found, was prophecy; he could correctly predict the future.

We lost a lot. We lost our first two games by a combined score of—I'm not kidding here—60-0. Over the season, we lost by an average score of 20-4.

Despite such lopsided games, I will never forget that first season, snippets of which I offer here, culled from a journal I kept during the nine weeks:

May 5: I never realized 11- and 12-year-olds asked so many questions:

"Where's the bathroom?"

"What color will our uniforms be?"

"When is the first game?"

"Why is the field so bumpy?"

"Why is there only one bat?"

"What kind of mileage does your Datsun B-210 get?"

One kid wanted to know if we could have Farrah Fawcett-Majors iron-ons to decorate the back of our jerseys.

The Prophet may be right: We might lose a lot. It's just a feeling I have.

May 12: Our catcher is the biggest character on the team. He's not much larger than a 32-ounce bat and has never caught before. The equipment hangs on him like a Charlie Brown Christmas tree with oversized ornaments.

He's a feisty, mischievous kid, a Dennis-the-Menace type who says what's on his mind. After he muffed a play today, I gave him two laps for saying what was on his mind. But for some reason I can't help but like the guy.

May 19: Our first game was one of those good news/bad news events. The good news: Our pitcher threw a no-hitter. The bad news: We lost 7-3. Control is not his forte. He walked 13 batters.

May 24: Our first pitcher walked eight batters and we fell behind 10-0 after the first inning. (We had only one out at that point but the ump ended the inning because of the 10-run rule.)

The catcher went out to the mound to discuss things with the pitcher. When the meeting was over, the pitcher looked shaken. After the inning was over, the shortstop came to me.

"Coach," he said, "you'd better do something about our catcher."

Our catcher? Wouldn't it be more appropriate to do something about our pitcher, the guy who kept giving opponents the get-on-base-free cards?

"Our catcher?" I said.

"Yeah, he came out to the mound and told Billy he was going to punch him in the nose if he didn't start throwing strikes."

The game was called after three innings. We lost 33-0. Tonight I found myself checking the schedule to see when our last game is. I circled it on my calendar, the way you would circle Christmas or a vacation or something else that couldn't come soon enough.

May 31: After losing 27-0 and 13-2, the team's morale has begun to sink. The players don't mind losing, it's losing without uniforms that bothers them so much. In addition, they wish they could have a jug of Kool-Aid on the bench like other teams.

June 6: The uniforms arrive. I'm hoping the additional team pride will help us play better.

June 7: I think I hoped for the impossible. We lost 21-0 today. But I must admit, we looked sharp doing so. And we're rarely thirsty on our journey to defeat. We have Kool-Aid now.

Our catcher, I've noticed, carries on a running conversation with the plate umpire, the batter, and, sometimes, the fans. Today the umpire politely told him that if he spoke again, he would drop-kick the young man over second base. For the first time, he shut up.

June 20: Our losing streak has increased to seven games. I was putting away the gear after today's 25-3 loss when a little boy who had apparently watched the game rolled up on his bicycle.

"Mister, are you the coach of that team that lost today?" he said.

"I sure am," I said, half-expecting a word of encouragement.

"That's too bad," he said, and rode away.

July 5: We're getting better. An umpire today told me we were the most improved team in the league. We've dropped 12 straight now.

I've made some coaching errors and the kids have made some playing errors, but our fans have remained loyal— even the shortstop's mom, who has to keep the scorebook for games like our 33-0 loss that involved 23 errors and 41 stolen bases. It is a herculean task, like keeping minutes at a school board meeting that turns into a brawl.

A team with a 19-1 lead stole home on us. An old season is getting older.

Right now, our magic number is eight: eight more days until the season is over. Two more games. Tomorrow's is against the other expansion team, the only team in the league that we've held to fewer than 13 runs.

"How many of you think we can win tomorrow?" I asked at the end of practice. Every player's hand shot up without hesitation. I didn't know whether to laugh or cry.

July 6: Today I laughed. We all laughed. Because we did it. We finally won a game. Coaches are never supposed to show a lack of confidence. They're supposed to say things like "never say die" and "winners never quit and quitters never win." But as we took the field in the bottom of the last inning with an 8-6 lead, I was the "ye of little faith" poster boy.

I was scared. Scared because in 59 innings during the season, only six times had we held our opponents to less than two runs. One in 10 odds. But now, that's what we had to do to win.

What happened next was something that hadn't happened all season. Our pitcher, Brian, struck out all three batters. Just like that. As if he'd done it all season long.

For an instant, I just stood there like a caged animal set free, not knowing quite what to do, having never known what freedom was.

Some of the players leapt for joy. The shortstop had tears in his eyes. I joined in the celebration, which shifted to the A&W when the first baseman's father said the drinks were on him.

Our catcher took a long pull on his root beer, then looked over at me. "Hey coach," he said, his face smudged with dirt from the mask, "we finally winned one."

"Yeah, we did," I said. "We winned one."

It was the lead item in the Little League baseball roundup the next day in our town's newspaper. That's not too surprising, considering I was the sports editor of that paper and wrote the article myself, though I did have the ethical tact to not interview and quote myself.

July 13: In the final game of the season, our winning streak was halted at one. But, oh, what a winning streak it was: short, but like any time in life when we find the light after a long period of darkness, so very, very sweet.

Hot Box

I was pounding in bases, preparing for the first practice with the new seventh-grade team I would be coaching, and feeling good for a couple of reasons:

First, it was May, meaning the base spikes would bore through the soggy Oregon soil with ease; by August, those same spikes would look like stainless steel curly fries, humbled by rock-hard dirt that had all the give of Hoover Dam.

Second, tryout week was over. I hate tryout week. In only three practices, you must select the best 15 baseball players out of about 50 kids. That's the easy part. The hard part is breaking the hearts of 35 players and about three times that many parents and stepparents and grandparents, some of whom think you're some sort of magic genie who can make their dreams come true. One year, a couple of boys were so upset at not being chosen that they bicycled by one of our practices with a paintball gun and nailed our left-fielder in the leg.

Ah, but that was all behind me now. The teams had been divided, the players had been notified, and it was time to start grooming this squad for the season ahead.

Suddenly, as I hammered the last peg at second base, a shadow appeared next to me. Turning, I realized it belonged to a man I knew—a man I knew whose son's dream hadn't come true. I had cut his kid.

"Well, you really blew it this time, Welch," said the man, his voice laced with venom.

The worst moment in journalism is when you're reading a story you've written and realize you've made an error. You've done someone irreparable harm. You think, momentarily, of all those tens of thousands of papers that are on people's doorsteps with your mistake in it, and you get this feeling in the pit of your stomach, the "I-wish-I'd-been-a-milkman" feeling that hearkens back to those college days when you were going to bag the pressure of journalism for the simplicity of delivering milk, a job whose biggest screwup might mean someone eats their Frosted Flakes with skim instead of 2%.

That's how I felt when the man said I'd blown it—like I'd made some terrible mistake.

"How many years has my son made your team? Now this. This is just great. His brother gets cut from his team last night. Now this. Thanks a bunch."

I didn't say anything, just started walking toward first base to hammer down the final bag. My silence was partly because I didn't know what to say and partly because I'm the nonconfrontive sort. But I felt like I'd been kicked in the gut. This was a man who'd been an assistant coach for me in years past, a guy who'd kept our team's scorebook.

"I thought newspaper reporters were supposed to be objective," the man said. "Not in this case. You seemed a little biased toward your son's friends."

My heart was pounding. The guy wasn't letting up. Do I just let it go?

I let it go. I said nothing, just began pounding in the first-base bag.

"I hope you're proud of yourself," he huffed in conclusion. "I hope you can sleep tonight."

And off he stomped.

Maybe he was right; maybe I had blown it. Maybe I had been biased. Maybe I wouldn't sleep tonight.

But in the weeks to come, I confirmed within myself that I'd made the right decision; it was his problem, not mine. I told the story to friends of mine, who assured me I was right and the man was wrong. Still, the criticism stung.

I don't like relationships with untied knots; "If it is possible, as far as it depends on you, live at peace with everyone," says Romans 12:18.

Looking back, I can think of only a few people with whom I've had falling-outs that haven't healed. But reconciliation didn't look likely with this rift.

Maybe I should call this guy and politely but firmly speak my mind. Tell him he'd wounded me. Explain why I'd made the choice I'd made. See if he might be willing to apologize so we could let it go.

But I didn't.

Occasionally, I'd see the man—he was helping coach his son's team—at the practice field. He avoided me. I avoided him. It was like that all summer long, two grown men seeing one another and pretending not to, each of us probably wondering what the other was thinking. It wore on me, week in and week out. And what bothered me more was that it probably wasn't wearing on him; otherwise, I figured, he would have called and apologized.

Maybe I should quit this silly coaching stuff, I thought. I'd been doing it for a decade. I didn't need this kind of friction; didn't need this guilt that I kept feeling, as if I were some ruthless king who had purposely denied a pauper's dream.

But I didn't. I finished the season, laughed at the team pizza party, dutifully turned in our team's equipment, and returned to my post-baseball life. School started, followed by Oregon's famous winter rains, which seemed to wash away the memory of the confrontation.

That's all I needed, I realized: Time. Distance. Distractions. Stuff that would help me forget about something that had already cost me more mental hand-wringing than it deserved. Let him deal with it; it was his problem.

And that's exactly what happened: Work. Deadlines. Thanksgiving. Launching a book. Such stuff helped shove the incident far back in my mind's attic, back behind the Christmas tree ornaments and children's toys, so I could forget about it.

Until the morning of Christmas Eve. That's when our pastor gave a message that brought it all back, but in a new light. He spoke, naturally, about the birth of Christ. About God's Son come to earth. About a humble peasant girl, great with child, who trusted that God was behind all this. About this Christ child being God's way of reconciling with man, His gift, given unconditionally for us, a bunch of sinners, including me.

So how, then, shall we live? the pastor asked. He flipped to 1 Peter 5:5. "All of you, clothe yourselves with humility toward one another, because God opposes the proud but gives grace to the humble."

Something stirred within me. We sang "O Little Town of Bethlehem" and something stirred even deeper, especially when I sang the lines:

> Yet in thy dark streets shineth
> The everlasting Light;
> The hopes and fears of all the years
> Are met in thee tonight

I've always loved those lines, but now they took on an added sense of urgency. That everlasting Light was shining in my attic, illuminating my own hopes and fears. The time, I realized, had come.

When we arrived home from church, I searched the phone book, found the man's name, and started to make the call. He's probably not home, I reasoned, and cradled the receiver.

Make the call.

I picked up the phone. But what was I going to say? I had no idea. I held the phone in both hands, undecided.

Make the call.

But he'll think I'm nuts. He won't even remember the incident. I'll be totally embarrassed.

Make the call.

I punched the number and mumbled a silent prayer; God deserved better.

The man's wife answered.

"It's Bob Welch," I heard her whisper to her husband. In the seconds before he came on the phone, I wondered what the mention of my name would trigger in him. Anger? Bitterness? Or maybe nothing. Maybe he hadn't thought about the incident since it happened, and the joke was on me, because it had eaten away at me like an ulcer for the last six months.

That's OK, I figured, because what mattered now wasn't his attitude, but mine. I'd once been to a Promise Keepers event in which an African-American man—a man who had been wronged in ways that made any incivilities against me seem trivial by comparison—said something so profound I've never forgotten it: At times someone will wrong you and your pride will preclude you from trying to reconcile with that person. You may even be clearly right and the other person clearly wrong.

"The question is this," he said: "Would you rather be right, or would you rather be reconciled?"

In a sense, we occasionally find ourselves in a relational hot box, a rundown between pride and humility. And pride is the base we naturally head for.

…Or would you rather be reconciled?

The seconds it took for the man to pick up the phone seemed like hours. But eventually he came on the line. Every now and then, God moves people to do things they could never do without Him, like those people you read about in *Reader's Digest* who summon the strength to lift a minivan that's crushing some little boy and then later have no idea how they did it.

That's what God did in this instance. What I told the man was nothing eloquent. It was stilted. It was jittery and jagged and came out of left field—a grown man telling another grown man, a guy he hardly knew, that he was sorry. That he'd just been to church and felt convicted to call and make things right. And that he'd made mistakes before in choosing teams, and probably would next year, too, and, well, he hoped the man would forgive him for not choosing his son last summer.

The man on the other end of the line dropped his guard. He told of how hurt his older son had been in not making the team he'd hoped to make; when the same thing happened to his younger son the next day, the man had snapped. He was sorry, too.

They were both sorry. It was Christmas Eve.

"Merry Christmas," I said.

"And Merry Christmas to you," he said.

❖ ❖ ❖

Before the next season began, I'd already decided it would be my last year of coaching. My younger son, whose team I had coached for five years, would be in the high school program, and others would coach him. The time had come to hang up the whistle—or at least take a long sabbatical.

But our last year together was a great year. We had a mediocre team but we played hard and pulled some big upsets. We beat one of those cocky teams with a coach who respects nobody, not even his own players. We won the consolation bracket championship. And we simply had fun, in part because of an assistant coach I'd invited to help me— the father of the boy I'd cut the previous year.

At times, during the season, I'd look over from my third-base box and see the man coaching first base, laughing, and giving base-running advice to my son, his son, and other people's sons—and I'd be reminded of one simple truth: the love of God can bore through hearts more resistant than a rock-hard infield in August.

The Old Gray-Haired Guy

Someone once asked me who I thought was the best coach I'd ever had the privilege to watch. I thought of John Wooden, who coached UCLA basketball teams to a record 10 NCAA titles in 12 years. I thought of Don Shula, the ex-Miami Dolphins' coach who won more games than anyone in NFL history. I thought of four-time NCAA Football Coach-of-the Year Joe Paterno of Penn State, who's won more college football games than anybody still coaching.

Then I thought of Steve Panter, a guy so obscure some of his neighbors probably don't even know him. Each November for the past 16 years, as the winter rains descend on Oregon, he pulls out a bag of basketballs from the trunk of his car, grabs his clipboard and ice pack, and walks into a middle-school gym whose door is always propped open by a rug, lest it lock.

Like thousands of other men and women across the country, Steve Panter coaches kids. But what separates him from so many is exactly that: he coaches kids. He doesn't use kids to fuel his selfish dreams. He doesn't turn kids into robo-warriors. He doesn't berate kids.

He teaches. He inspires. He leads. And does so with more compassion than anyone I've ever seen.

Now 50 and a grandfather, he calls himself "the old gray-haired guy," though racquetball and road biking keep him in solid shape. For most of his coaching career, he's taken the same eighth grade team—not the top-level players; instead, the ones who hoped to make the top team but didn't. He puts in about three months a year, four or five days a week. For that, he gets a five-dollars-off coupon for his child to play in the league, which is of little use since his two sons are grown.

His teams have made it to the city finals six times and claimed a city championship, so he knows how to win. But the true measure of a coach isn't found in city championships or in victories. It's not even found under the glare of gymnasium lights. Instead, it's found in the bond—or lack thereof—between coach and players.

❖ ❖ ❖

—It's found in a dimly lit hallway where a lanky forward slumps against the wall in anguish, having just missed a handful of layins that would have sealed a championship game. Instead, Panter's team lost by a point.

In the gym, the victors celebrated with gusto. Panter's team, meanwhile, wandered around like jet-crash victims, having been ahead by seven points with less than two minutes to go before their dream crashed and burned.

In such situations, I've seen losing coaches slam down clipboards. I've seen coaches speed-walk, head down, to the locker room. I've seen coaches head for an official like a heat-seeking missile. But what I saw this Sunday afternoon was a coach notice a lone player in a hallway, in tears.

I saw that coach put his arm around the young man, smile, and console him with words that did not come easy— I know Panter was hurting, too—but nevertheless came: Words that affirmed. "...without you, we never would have gotten close to the finals..." Words that encouraged, "...hurts now but trials like this will toughen you..." Words that enlightened. "...life is way more important than a basketball game...."

—It's found behind the school, where one of Panter's players had left a practice after a run-in with some teammates. Panter ran after the kid. He knew the general situation: the boy's parents were getting divorced and the kid had been handed off to grandparents. There was a sadness about him.

Panter asked the boy why he was leaving. "Neither of my parents want me," he said. "I'm living with my grandparents, and they don't want me either. Now some of the kids on the team just told me they don't want me. In the whole world, nobody wants me. I don't belong anywhere."

Panter knelt down and searched for words. The kid sobbed on his shoulder. Finally, the words just came: "John, I know a place where you belong—right here. I'm your coach and I want you on my team."

He remembers two things about what he told the kid: first, that the words seemed to have come down from On High—"What do you say to a kid in such despair?"—and, second, that they seemed to instantaneously ease the kid's pain.

Panter and the boy walked back to the team, which was practicing with an assistant coach. Panter stopped practice, gathered the players together, and explained what teams were all about: Togetherness. Respect. Forgiveness. "Everyone earned a spot on this team," he said. "Everyone belongs."

—It's found on a high school stage where a handful of seniors were being asked questions as part of a variety-show fundraiser.

One of the contestants was a "Panter kid" who had grown to nearly seven feet tall. Though six-foot-three even as an eighth grader, when he played for Panter he was too lazy to use his height. He wouldn't go to the hoop, wouldn't establish his presence, wouldn't be aggressive.

Once during practice, with Panter playing on the defensive team, the boy put up his usual lazy shot. The coach, 5-foot-11, leaped high, and blocked it with both hands. The boy fell on his back, more surprised than hurt.

From that point on, the kid became a basketball player. By late in his senior year of high school, he was among the league's best players. He also had among the league's hottest tempers, had gotten a few technical fouls, and had been suspended for a game.

About then, he ran into his old coach.

"What's going on?" Panter asked.

The player tried to rationalize his behavior. But just as he had five years ago, Panter blocked the shot with a verbal challenge. Didn't he remember what the old gray-haired guy had told him about how losing your temper on the court was an advantage to the opposition? About how it takes energy away from your game? About how life isn't always fair, and neither are some calls, but you can't waste your time complaining?

From that point, the kid's attitude started improving. He won a college scholarship. And there he was, the spring of his senior year, up on the stage, as the contest host asked, "What one person has had the most influence on your life to this point?"

He thought for only a moment.

"My eighth-grade basketball coach," he said.

❖ ❖ ❖

The Old Gray-Haired Guy was once a yeller and a screamer, he'll tell you, but the rafting accident in 1986 changed all that. Unconscious in the cold McKenzie River water for about five minutes—his head having hit a cooler or a rock—he'd come as close to death as he ever had. Before the accident, he'd known something was missing in his life;

he saw this as an icy wakeup call. He began trusting God, not himself, and, over time, noticed his priorities changing from getting his way to giving to others, from winning games to nurturing kids.

For Panter, basketball is not life; it's a part of life, a way to learn about life. He doesn't humiliate players who have made mistakes with words that hurt; instead, he'll tell them, "You just had a stupid attack. That doesn't mean you're bad, it just means you did something wrong."

He looks for the positive. He minimizes running drills and maximizes basketball; "It's a game," he says. "That means it's supposed to be fun."

He honestly believes the "…how-you-play-the-game" axiom, and abhors a league rule that says if one team gets ahead of another by more than 15 points, the free-standing scoreboard must be turned around so spectators can't see it.

"What that says to a coach and team is, 'You should be ashamed of yourselves. You're so bad we don't want people to see how much better the other team is than you.' Hogwash. If they're playing their hardest, that team should be proud of every point it gets. And what about that reserve who maybe gets his first basket of the season? Shouldn't he or she have the thrill of seeing those points be put on the board?"

He demands discipline: No swearing. No showboating. No failed classes. You play by the rules. You respect your opponent and the officials. And your coach and teammates.

But he leavens such demands with an allowance to be human. Sports are emotional, he'll tell his players; at times, you might feel like crying. So cry. Nothing to be ashamed of. Tears sometimes soothe the hurt.

He keeps his cool. In fact, the only time I've seen him flat-out mad was after a timekeeper clearly cheated so his son's team would have more time for a last-second shot to win—which is exactly what happened.

What incensed Panter wasn't that his team had lost, but that his players—kids—had been victimized by an adult who had ignored the rules of the game, who had sacrificed honor and fairness to the god of greed: winning.

Lots of coaches talk about their bottom lines being kids. Panter's truly is. He occasionally starts practices—after getting approval from parents—with a five-minute talk about attitude or drugs or sex. He has the courage to confront parents who push their kids too hard, including the father who charted his son's shots during tryouts so he could spot the boy's weaknesses. He gives his MVP awards to every kid on the team.

He tells the players at the final banquet that they're welcome to call him, day or night, any hour, if they're ever in trouble, need help, or just want someone to listen. And more than one has taken him up on the offer.

The oldest Panter player is now about 30. Every now and then, the coach will be at a restaurant or a game and he'll hear someone from behind say, "Hey, coach." And, more often than not, it will be a player who'll not only reminisce about the old team but also mention that he still has his MVP trophy or remembers that line about stupid attacks.

History will remember the Woodens, Shulas, and Paternos of the world—and well it should. But kids who play sports will remember the Steve Panters of their childhoods, the coaches who, for a five-dollars-off coupon, teach not just the game of basketball or soccer or hockey, but the life stuff that lasts.

Wounded Sparrows

Are not two sparrows sold for a penny? Yet not one of them will fall to the ground apart from the will of your Father. And even the very hairs of your head are all numbered. So don't be afraid; you are worth more than many sparrows.

—Matthew 10: 29-31

The first basketball team I coached was at an elementary school so small that even when combining the fourth and fifth grades, I had to do some extensive recruiting just to have five starters. The country school had fewer students in its entire student body, 65, than my boys had had in their respective grades in the suburban school from which they'd transferred.

It was a bittersweet year. I recall walking out of the gym on a snowy night—rare for the rainy Willamette Valley—and driving slowly home on a country road with Ryan and Jason, thinking life doesn't get much better than being the first car on a snowy road after a good basketball practice with your two sons in back, talking about sledding the next day.

But I also recall learning that one of my players had a painful past. Shortly before the season, the kid's father had pulled his van off a country road one night, pulled out a gun, and shot himself in the head.

I realize this is a jolting image when juxtaposed with pictures of snow-covered country roads, but the memory reminds me that the children we, as coaches, are charged with often arrive at practice with painful pasts—and painful presents—that we dare not ignore.

Whether we coach for a five-room country school or an urban youth league, we're responsible for children with baggage. Children who come from, and go back to, homes where hurt is a way of life. Children looking for something—even if they're not sure just what.

We may offer them a couple of hours of calm in lives that are otherwise catastrophic, stability in a sea of inconsistency, encouragement in a world where they get little. Once, at a coaches' clinic, the leader said something I'll never forget: "As a coach, you may sometimes feel insignificant. But remember this: For some kids, you may be the only person all week who makes them feel like they're worth anything at all."

I wonder if some coaches understand what a crucial role they can play in the life of a child. I can think of a few coaches I've seen who did not, including the baseball coach who yanked his shortstop in mid-inning, right after the kid made an error; it was, he later said, for the good of the team. Ten years later, when that humiliation still haunts the kid's subconscious, will it still seem like the best decision?

Some coaches underestimate how pivotal they can be in the lives of their players—not only in teaching them how to shoot a jump shot, but in how to believe in themselves. In how to be part of a team. In how to bounce back from defeat.

I look at my old team photos and I can still account for most of the kids, even though some of them are now more than six inches taller than me. In fact, since my team broke up two years ago and the kids started high school, I've written them each summer with a small word of encouragement, like a mother whose babe is heading off to camp for the first time. But a few come back Address Unknown.

News of them comes third-hand.

"Heard he moved to California to live with his father again."

"Someone said he was in the juvenile facility."

"On the streets, I think."

I see their faces in the team photos—the kids here and there who drifted away as the teenage years hit: troubled kids who would never say it aloud, but were desperately seeking someone to believe in them.

At the time, did I step to the plate to be that someone?

I think of these kids like I think of the homeless: How did they get this way? Where do they sleep? Where do they go from here? Who watches out for them? I realize help is a two-way street. Offering it isn't always enough; it must be accepted.

And some boys I coached had hearts so hardened that it seemed nothing would penetrate that protective shield—not encouragement, not praise, not challenge. In such dilemmas, coaches find themselves like the father and minister in Norman Maclean's *A River Runs Through It* who laments not being able to help his troubled younger son. How do you reach someone, he ponders, who doesn't want to be reached?

I recall the boy whose father once dropped him off at a game and went to play tavern darts with a girlfriend—and missed his son's game-winning hit in the third extra inning.

I recall the boy who didn't even know who his father was, and never stayed in one place long enough to establish any sense of security.

And I recall the boy whose life was shattered one evening by gunfire and the discovery that his father was dead, slumped over in the family car.

At the newspaper where I work, I was editing high school graduation lists recently and was encouraged to see that the young man made it through high school. Given the pain he's borne since that tragic night, graduating from high school seems like an accomplishment no less amazing than single-handedly breaking a full-court press.

With my sons now in college and high school, I've taken a break from coaching. Someday, though, I'd like to return, perhaps pick up a group of ragamuffins who can't find a coach. If I do, I need to remember the boy whose father killed himself, even if it isn't a pretty thought.

Need to be there for that kid who isn't getting much attention at home, knowing—as the clinic guy had said—that I might be the only one.

Need to remember that, though the team photos always show 15 smiling children in matching uniforms, such photos sometimes hide the lives behind—like black ice beneath a snowy country road.

The Armchair Quarterback

❖ ❖ ❖

They watch from afar. The thinkers. Those who would try to make sense of this thing called sports. Those who would try to examine beyond two teams, two scores, one field. They hypothesize. They scrutinize. They philosophize. All in an effort to understand the game beyond the game. They are the armchair quarterbacks.

Essence of the Game

Each year, millions of dollars go into the staging of—and hyping of—the Super Bowl. The halftime entertainment alone is a seven-digit extravaganza. This, combined with ad nauseam pre-game interviewing of players and coaches, serves as a prelude to what's supposed to be the highlight: the game itself.

But more often than not, the game is a dud, rarely being decided in the final seconds, rarely offering scintillating individual performances, and rarely creating the memorable mortar on which sports legends are built. In fact, the watercooler talk the next morning is less often about the game itself than about the highly creative commercials that interspersed the "action." (Just how *did* Pepsi make that mid-air refueling involving the geese look so real?)

However, during Oregon's winter drought of 1976-77 when I was 22 years old, a friend and I drove to a frozen lake high in the Cascade Mountains and, for the price of a 49-cent can of tuna fish that we used for a puck, faced off in a two-man hockey game that I still consider one of the absolutely legendary athletic events in the history of time. (As I recall, our halftime show consisted of eating a couple of bananas and watching an osprey commute to and from its treetop home.)

This is one thing I love about sports: its pleasures can't be bought, only discovered. The seventh game of the World Series may be exciting—so, on occasion, may the Super Bowl—but a Wiffle ball game at the Gonzales family reunion, in the eyes of at least the Gonzaleses, may be just as good or better. So may the first soccer goal kicked by a 7-year-old. Or the first 10K race run by a 70-year-old.

I recently saw a TV special on Kenya, where children routinely run from place to place and where the country's distance runners now dominate the world. What impressed me most was not so much the success they've found, but the pure joy they seem to have found in getting there. They seem untainted by big money, sponsorships, and greed.

Their embracing of sport seems to reflect life at its deepest level, unlike in America, where the essence of sports is clouded by greed.

I've watched professional golf tournaments where participants seem oblivious to the idea that they're actually involved in "sport," an activity for which Webster's Dictionary asks the reader to "see FUN."

At the 1998 PGA Golf Championships outside Seattle, Washington, my sons and I stationed ourselves behind the second green and watched every player in the final round come through. Granted, this is how these guys make their livings—I understand the need to concentrate—but let's be realistic: players who make the cut in the PGA aren't sinking putts so they can stay off food stamps. So why did the final round look like a death march with caddies?

How ironic that the one event in which U.S. golfers finally looked like they were actually having fun—their come-from-behind victory in the 1999 Ryder Cup—was an event for which they received no compensation whatsoever.

But the kind of youthful exuberance displayed by the Ryder Cup team—admittedly, a bit beyond the bounds of sportsmanship, but still refreshing—is the exception, not the rule. To watch a mid-season NBA game—as I did in Portland recently—is to watch sports with no soul: millionaires oozing with talent but loafing until the game's final minutes; players whining—"Who, me?"—when called for an obvious foul; and the incessant "ca-ching" of a cash register over the P.A. system when someone scores, a desperate attempt to inject life into a game with so little.

Could it be that the essence of sports is obscured by fame and fortune?

The glory of sports is that they are equal-opportunity activities whose pleasures are available to rich and poor, men and women, young and old. All sports require is people willing to step to the plate, toe the line, take the field. From that point, an athletic event becomes whatever it will become, regardless of who's playing, where it's being played, and what's at stake.

The appeal of sports is the unknown. You begin with this blank canvas and begin splashing on colors of paint—the hues of heart, desire, preparedness, skill, finesse, strategy, weather, venue, and chance. You begin with this sheet of ice and two goals made of rocks and a can of tuna fish—or, as I recently experienced, with the Seattle Mariners' new $517 million stadium complete with a retractable roof. You agree to a set of rules. And you play ball.

The thrill of sports is anticipation:

…Watching a 5-iron shot make its journey toward the green and not knowing if it will land soft and snuggle to the pin or hit hard and embed itself like a fried egg in the bunker.

…Watching a throw home from center field and not knowing if it will beat the runner trying to score from second or fly over the catcher's head.

…Watching a soccer player break toward the goal and not knowing if she'll score or get pick-pocketed by an opponent before she even has a chance to shoot.

Observing a good sports event—or participating in it—is like being involved in one of those mystery dinners in which the plot is being invented even as the event unfolds. As such, sports become a microcosm of life itself, snack packs of the agony and defeats we experience in the often-ragged world beyond the neatly chalked lines: Joy. Sorrow. Brilliance. Frustration. Dreams. And broken dreams. It's all there, the line between the bitter and the sweet at times painfully thin.

My older son's baseball team was one out from being eliminated in a playoff game when one of his light-hitting teammates came to the plate in the bottom of the last inning. The team was down by one. The boy had rarely hit even in normal situations; with the entire season on the line, nothing suggested he would suddenly become Mr. Clutch. But the crowd erupted as he poked a single to keep the team's hopes alive.

I turned to the boy's father, sitting behind me. "Whose son was that?" I said, loud enough for people nearby to hear.

No sooner had I spoken the words than I heard a loud voice yell, "Yer out." I spun around. The man's son, a bit cocky after his unlikely hit, had been picked off first base while leading off. Inning over. Game over. Season over. Just like that. Just like life.

I marvel at athletes who make clutch plays, in part because I was never that guy. I was never Brandi Chastain, who, in the summer of 1999, stood in the Rose Bowl in front of more than 90,000 fans and a record TV audience with one shot to win the World Cup against China. Because of the attention on this game, it was arguably the biggest moment in the history of women's sports. And she made the shot.

Yet what fascinates me is that the joy of making a goal like that is every bit as available to some 11-year-old girl who's playing in front of perhaps only 37 fans, including a mom who went into work at 6 A.M. so she could get off in time for the game. In that little girl's mind, her winning kick may be no less significant than Brandi Chastain's.

It's becoming more common to see professional athletes "hold out" for more money despite being offered contracts in excess of $10 million. When I think of such athletes, I think of a man in our church named Bob Daniels.

Recently, he won a handful of gold medals at a state Special Olympics skiing event, stood in front of our congregation to be honored, and beamed a smile that wouldn't end. The congregation clapped and clapped and clapped. And Bob, holding up his medals, smiled and smiled and smiled.

I can't help but think that between himself and the athletes for whom $10 million is not enough, he is the richer man.

America

I met him at a neighborhood Fourth of July barbecue. The host had each of us stand and tell something about ourselves. We told of our jobs, our families, our hobbies—the usual stuff.

Then it was his turn, the stocky man with the thick mustache and the strange accent who lived next door to us in Bellevue, Washington. He told of his job, his family, his hobbies—the usual stuff.

"And," said Boris Moskalensky, "I'm proud to be an American."

I had seen plenty of Fourth of July barbecues before. I had seen all the trappings—flags and fireworks, burgers and baseball. But until that moment, I had never seen anyone stand up and say he was proud to be an American.

On Independence Day 1988, the neighbors in our cul-de-sac taught Boris Moskalensky how to play baseball and slap a high-five. And Boris Moskalensky taught us how to appreciate something that many of us had taken for granted: a place called America.

The difference between Boris and his neighbors was clear. We had never known the flipside to the independence we so casually celebrated. But Boris had lived under communist rule for 42 years. Until coming to America, he had never known the freedom he had come to embrace so fervently.

He told us that people growing up in America didn't understand what it's like not to be free. He told us he knew the difference because, as he put it, he had spent 42 years in jail. Or running from those who wanted him in jail.

As we gathered round, he told stories of the Hungarian Revolution in 1956. Of working for the Soviet military. Of seeing trainloads of wounded soldiers returning from battle. And of thinking, for the first time, that his country was evil.

The Hungarians, he said, just wanted a new way to live. They were not Fascists. They were just people, looking for something better than they had. As were Boris and his family in the years to come.

He began questioning his country more and more. He began listening to American broadcasts on short-wave radio and realized there was another way to live. He realized he lived in a country that regularly lied to him.

In the late '70s, the Soviets loosened their emigration policy and Boris made his decision: he and his family would try to come to America. Word got out. His wife was fired from her job as a chemistry lab assistant. His son, a top student, was kicked out of school; the authorities said the boy was the son of a traitor.

Finally, the papers came. Permission was granted. But two weeks before they were to leave, Boris and Susana were confronted by two men who began bad-mouthing his wife. Boris readied his fists, but he knew the trap. Knew who they were: the KGB. Knew the stories of how they would instigate a fight, throw the husband in jail for assault, and leave him there for years, snuffing any dreams of departing for a better place.

But Boris refused to give up on that dream. Finally, after much more waiting and worrying, they were given clearance to leave. They moved to Seattle. What they found was the fresh air of freedom—and people who took much for granted.

He found it unbelievable that, just from studying for his citizenship test, he knew more about the country's history than many Americans who were born here.

He found it unbelievable that an election might draw only half of all registered voters.

He found it unbelievable that the country spends so much on welfare. Once, when the auto store Boris worked at went out of business, friends told him to go on welfare. He refused. I didn't do anything for this country, he said, why should they feel obligated to do something for me?

During the Olympic Games, people asked him if it was hard to decide who he wanted to win. Not at all, he would tell them. Russia is a country, he would say. The U.S. is *my* country.

You want to know the difference between the Soviet Union and America, he asked: Watch when they raise the flag for the Olympic champions. The Americans will have tears in their eyes, he said, because they are proud of their country. The Russians will not, because winning to them means only a better life. A job. But not pride for their country.

After the barbecue, as dusk descended, the folks in the neighborhood took to the middle of the cul-de-sac for a game of baseball. Boris had never played the game before and we taught him to field, bat, and speak "infield"—"hey, batta, batta, hey, batta, batta, swing!"

I will never forget what happened the first time he stepped to the plate. He swung mightily time after time after time. Nothing but air. Finally, he connected, a dribbler back to the pitcher. Boris dropped his bat and started running. He was out at first but seemed oblivious to that reality. Instead, he rounded first, raced to second, and headed for third.

My goodness, I realized: We had forgotten to teach him about running the bases and what constitutes an out. At first we hooted and hollered and politely pointed out that he was out, but Boris kept chugging, so we all just stopped shouting and eagerly watched. And smiled.

Boris rounded third and headed for the plate. He had a huge smile on his face, like a man who had been running his whole life, and was finally coming home.

14

Unquenchable Thirst

The most fascinating interview I've ever had with an athlete was with Alberto Salazar, at one time the greatest marathoner on earth. We sat in the living room of his home, Casa de Salazar, perched high on a hill overlooking much of the city of Eugene, the self-proclaimed running capital of the world.

What made it so fascinating was that Salazar, nearly a decade after winning three straight New York Marathons and breaking the Boston Marathon record, dared to bare his soul about the most profound part of sports: winning.

In two afternoons of interviews—he was also the most accommodating big-name athlete I've interviewed—Salazar revealed something that astounded me: at the peak of his career, when he could run 26 miles, 385 yards faster than any human being on the planet, Alberto Salazar was a man in anguish.

Self-driven to succeed, he could not be content without being the best—but neither could he be content after becoming the best. He was a man who seemingly created his own destiny, then watched it crumble. A man whose lack of peace gnawed at him like a runner's cramp that wouldn't go away.

Winning, it seems, was never enough. "It was a cycle," he said, looking back. "The more I achieved, the more I wanted. There was always one more step. Even if I won an NCAA championship, I'd say, 'Now I'll get a gold medal, now I'll set a world record, or now I'll beat the world record.' "

Whereas most runners rest in the days following a big race, Salazar would hit the road the next morning for 20 hard miles. He once put in a 100-mile-a-week summer—with a stress fracture. If Salazar ran 10,000 meters in 27 minutes and 45 seconds, it didn't matter that he'd won and set a meet record; if he was shooting for 27:30, he would smile his way around a few victory laps, then enter the locker room seething. "I would hate that. I would feel I failed."

❖ ❖ ❖

Winning is the great paradox of sports. Whether reflected in the Super Bowl or a coach-pitch youth game, American culture views being No. 1 as a sacred achievement, the ultimate goal, the main reason we compete. But with all due respect to the late Vince Lombardi, winning isn't everything.

Winning is a worthy goal; a summer doesn't pass that I don't drive past the Shasta Middle School ball fields and picture my younger son's last-inning poke to center field, wishing that the outfielder hadn't made a diving catch to thwart our comeback attempt and end the championship game, 4-2.

Winning is much more fun than losing. I should know; I played on a City League basketball team that went 0-for-three-years, though we did take a team into overtime before losing our 30th and last game.

But in itself, winning isn't enough; the cost-to-benefit ratio is too high. It can't compensate for children so stressed by sports that they grind their teeth at night. Parents so intent on turning their children into superstars that they sacrifice the family in the process. And athletes so obsessed with being the best that it carries over into their nonathletic life.

In their book, *Winning and Other American Myths*, psychologist Thomas Tutko and writer William Bruns put it in terms to which Alberto Salazar could relate:

> Winning is like drinking salt water; it will never quench your thirst. It is an insatiable greed. There are never enough victories, never enough championships or records....

There's a difference between giving an all-out effort to win and being obsessed with winning.

Winning has become an obsession when a Babe Ruth baseball coach—as happened in my fair city recently—is caught using a college-aged assistant coach as a designated hitter.

Winning has become an obsession when a Little League coach in southern Oregon gives his players $5 for every base hit in an all-star game.

Winning has become an obsession when, midway through a season, a team—like one I saw recently—loses its desire to even play because they've been made to feel like such failures by their win-or-else coach.

We are becoming an increasingly results-oriented, rather than process-oriented, culture. Outcome has become everything; the experience has become nothing.

Once, while coaching youth baseball, our team got trounced in a game that, according to league rules, had to be called after four innings because the margin was 10 runs. The umpires left. Parents started to leave.

I was stunned: In essence, we were saying that a baseball game has no value unless it is close; that it's so humiliating to be behind by 10 runs that it's better to not continue the very reason these kids turned out in the first place: to play. To have fun. To compete.

As people headed for their cars, I thought about how my team had worked hard all week in practice and had been rewarded by this: a rule that said you can't play because you're not good enough. I grabbed two parents who agreed to be umpires, went to the other coach, and suggested we keep playing—with the understanding, of course, that officially the game was over and his team had won 12-2.

He shrugged and said OK. Most parents returned to their seats. A parent-turned-umpire called "play ball" and one of the opposing team's batters stepped into the box.

Then the batter said something that has haunted me ever since. "Coach," he yelled to the burly man in the third-base box. "Are we just playing for fun now?"

I've never heard a sadder commentary on children and sports in my life. As adults, we should be ashamed when we allow sports to become so win-oriented that young people think the "fun light" only goes on once their game or practice is over. The "fun light" should go on the minute their game or practice begins; because fun—pure, unadulterated play— is the truest essence of sports. Otherwise, let's just call it war or business or politics or something worse.

On the flip side, one of the most beautiful moments I've ever seen in sports came at the tail-end of a recent high school girls' basketball game. The two teams had traded one-point leads for nearly the entire fourth quarter and finally two guards who had been dogging each other all night wound up going one-on-one. Three…two…one…The offensive player fired a do-or-die shot to win the game. It missed.

Then, the moment: The two girls, both physically and emotionally spent, instinctively hugged each other—as if sports for them went far beyond which red bulbs were lit up on a scoreboard, went to something deeper, something in the soul: in this case, respect for one another and, perhaps, pride in a battle well fought.

I think that's how God sees sports, too. I think He sees beyond two numbers when the game is over. From a human perspective, winning—be it in the form of accumulating material goods, achieving recognition, or amassing power—is everything. From God's perspective, relating is everything. At least that's what Jesus told a Pharisee when asked what the most important commandment was: to love God with all your heart, soul, and mind, and to love your neighbor as yourself.

My point isn't that we shouldn't strive to win; in Philippians, Paul encourages us to "press on toward the goal to win the prize for which God has called me heavenward in Christ Jesus." But that prize is not some temporal trophy that we earn through strategy and hard work; the prize is everlasting life and isn't earned, period. It's a gift. "For it is by grace you have been saved, through faith—and this not from yourselves, it is the gift of God—not by works..." (Ephesians 2:8).

I believe God is glorified more when a group of football players humbly congratulate their winning opponents than when they bow in prayer before a potentially game-winning field goal. God, says Matthew, "causes his sun to rise on the evil and the good, and sends rain on the righteous and the unrighteous" (Matthew 5:45). I think He's less concerned whether we win or lose than how we react when we're winning or losing—and how we react when we've won or lost.

I recently saw a young man slide into third and accidentally spike the third baseman in the knee. Moments later, he helped carry his opponent to the dugout. That young man saw beyond the scoreboard.

A friend and I ran a 10K road run recently. We agreed before the race that we would run the first half together, then go our separate ways if one was feeling stronger than the other. At the halfway mark, I pulled away. But near the finish, he passed me, gave me a word of encouragement, and wound up finishing ahead of me. A few days later, he walked into my office with a jar of homemade strawberry jam. "You pulled me along for most of the race," he said. "Thanks." He saw beyond the stopwatch.

My son was coaching a youth sports playoff game that went into overtime. In the extra period, I was surprised to see him put in the shortest, least-skilled player for a few minutes. After the game, which his team had won, I questioned him about the move.

"It's just a YMCA basketball game, Dad," he said. "The kid hadn't gotten to play, so I put him in." My son saw beyond wins and losses.

Winning feels good. It's comfortable. But God is less concerned about our comfort than he is about our character.

If winning were God's priority, why does he allow the rain to fall on the righteous and the unrighteous? Why not just the righteous?

If winning were God's priority, why did Jesus hang out with so many people whom society considered losers? And why did he reserve so much of his wrath for the Pharisees, the folks whom society considered the winners?

If winning were God's priority, why did he allow his own son to die on a cross? In the world's eyes, wasn't that the ultimate loss?

We live in a winning-is-everything culture but serve a winning-isn't-everything God. We need to transcend the values of our times.

Competition is the hub on which the athletic wheel turns. But we are to compete for the right reasons—not out of a sense of personal glory or revenge or fear or anger, but for his glory.

What's important here isn't our perfection, but our purpose. I once wrote a letter to encourage a friend, a coach whose enthusiasm for the game seemed gone, his frustration at losing manifesting itself in uncharacteristic fits of courtside rage.

"Sometimes I get so caught up in the race," he wrote back, "that I forget why I entered."

Sometimes, it takes a child to remind us that it's the journey, not the outcome or stopwatch, that matters most. At an all-comers track meet in Eugene, a 7-year-old finished fourth in the 220-yard dash.

"How fast did you run?" asked an adult.

"As fast as I could," he replied, eyes wide.

What profundity. As adults, I wish we could see so clearly. Wish we could see that we need to rethink our approach to sports. Wish we could see what we've created when a 12-year-old boy steps into the batter's box, turns to his coach, and, in essence, asks if it's OK to have fun.

15

Frog

He was the new kid at Garfield School, a sixth-grader who had just moved from Idaho. Given that state's abundance of a certain type of vegetable and our group's sense of humor and provinciality, we toyed with the idea of calling him "Mr. Potato Head." Based on his thick, black glasses, however, we settled instead on simply "Frog." I don't recall his doing anything in particular to offend us. Nor do I recall our blatantly bullying him.

I just recall subtly reminding him early on that we were here first and, thus, better than him.

Until, that is, he came out for flag football practice and we realized the kid had a cannon for an arm, was lightning fast, and knew football like Hershey's knows chocolate. He certainly didn't look the part—he looked, well, kind of nerdy in those glasses. But anyone who could help us win football games was good enough for us; we offered him membership in our exclusive club.

I thought of "Frog" in the wake of the shootings at Columbine High School in Colorado. I thought of how easily we label people without even knowing them, particularly if we're insiders and, like "Frog," they're outsiders. I thought of how quick we are—even as adults—to decide who belongs in the inner circle and who does not.

Finally, I thought of how the Columbine killers specifically singled out jocks as targets. Their thinking? You've bullied us, ridiculed us, humiliated us. But, surprise, we bat last. They then stepped to the plate and began swinging unmercifully.

Nothing—absolutely nothing—justifies the bloody rampage that ensued. Nothing excuses murder. Nothing rationalizes the tragedy that 15 people are dead and the lives of those who knew them and loved them will never be the same. But amid such tragedy, we're negligent if, instead of pointing fingers at others, we don't also look in the mirror and try to learn something.

I realize it's a long way from a minor snub at Garfield School in the '60s to gunfire at Columbine High in the '90s, and yet the incidents touch on sports and exclusivity—who belongs and who does not.

As much as sports can bring together communities and individuals, they can also build walls between the perceived "haves" and "have-nots." At Columbine, the state wrestling champ was regularly permitted to park his $100,000 Hummer all day in a 15-minute space, the homecoming king was on probation for burglary, and a football player was allowed to tease a girl in class without fear of retribution by his teacher, also the boy's coach.

As much as sports can produce the kind of heroes we desperately need, many athletes and coaches in America are accorded a place of honor that they don't deserve—pampered and indulged not because of any particular character quality, but because they can hit a curve ball or throw a tight spiral, or coach a basketball team to a conference title.

As much as sports can teach lessons such as honesty, commitment, and teamwork, so can they teach lessons of arrogance, selfishness, and bigotry. When I was in high school, a bunch of jocks and one journalist/jock (me) were riding in a car one winter evening, firing icy snowballs at oncoming cars. When one smacked like a rock into the windshield of a car, I said "Enough!" We needed to stop; someone was going to get hurt. My friends just laughed, so I got out of the car and walked a mile home in the dark.

Years later, the incident would remind me that power turns ugliest when it's the result of majority-rules thinking based solely on concern for one's self. It leads to countries starting wars. It leads to high school cliques bullying those who don't belong. It leads to racism and sexism. And sometimes, it leads to the kind of self-righteous thinking that angered Jesus like nothing else.

He hated the idea of people lording power over others. Wrote the apostle Paul:

> Do nothing out of selfish ambition or vain conceit, but in humility consider others better than yourselves. Each of you should look not only to your own interests, but also to the interests of others.
>
> Your attitude should be the same as that of Christ Jesus: Who, being in very nature God, did not consider equality with God something to be grasped, but made himself nothing, taking the very nature of a servant.
>
> —Philippians 2:3-7

The verses suggest honor and integrity have nothing to do with the group to which we belong and everything to do with our hearts. Translating that thinking to Garfield School, 1965, my pals and I would have accepted "Frog" whether or not he wore thick, black glasses, and whether or not he could throw a football. Instead, in a sense, he had to prove himself worthy of our acceptance.

A few years ago, I was asked to return to my old high school and speak to the newspaper class. A classmate of mine was on hand, too. We were two very different people— in high school, she had been part of what was called the

"Folk Dancers" clique, more apt to be spending a Friday night reading poetry or smoking pot than at a football game. When our presentations to the newspaper class were finished, we talked briefly about our high school days and how rigid had been the boundaries between groups.

"If I had to do it over again, I think it would have been fun to be in a play," I told her.

"Hey, I confess, I looked at everyone involved in Spirit Week and thought: That looks like fun."

But of course, The Rules wouldn't allow us such access to enemy camps—as if we were all dogs penned in by those invisible fences.

Our conversation was encouraging because it reminded me that people can change and grow and gain perspective. Looking back on my school days, I realize how painfully easy it was to pigeonhole people as this or that, without even knowing who they were. And how small-minded we were in according respect only to those who had proven to us, in our Pharisee-like arrogance, that they could further our cause.

I think of one young man named Mike Riley, who graduated from high school a year ahead of me. He was a jock, but not one of those who lorded that identity over anyone else. He was tremendously talented but equally humble and shy, a guy who helped lead our school to state titles in three sports, and yet remained this unassuming presence whose heart always seemed to be in the right place.

After high school, Riley played college football under the legendary Bear Bryant at Alabama and became a coach. In Canada, his Winnipeg teams won two Grey Cup titles, that country's equivalent of our Super Bowl, and then he coached in the United States Football League and at Southern California.

He then returned to Corvallis, where he'd spent much of his childhood, to become head coach at Oregon State. In two years, he breathed life back into a football program that had been on a ventilator since about the time Riley had started shaving.

He did so well that, after two years, he was hired as head coach of the San Diego Chargers, now makes $750,000 a year, and lives with his wife and children in what's arguably the most livable city in the NFL.

When I think of Mike Riley, I'm reminded that not all nice guys finish last. I'm also reminded that some people who like to think they're nice guys—people like me—need to remember that we all have a little Pharisee blood in us, and need to be careful about exalting ourselves while putting down those around us until they earn the keys to our clique.

Back at Garfield School, you see, we had a nickname for Mike Riley.

It was "Frog."

16

The Great Abyss

Every now and then, I have this dream or some variation of it: I'm standing on the first tee of a golf course, ready to tee off in this annual four-man golf tournament which I've been part of for 23 years. The first hole always looks like one of those drawings by the artists who draw devilish golf holes—a twisting par-5 on the side of Mount Everest or a par-3 with an island green surrounded by boiling water full of piranhas or a 700-yard par-4 with a fairway no wider than a hotel hallway.

I stand over the ball, preparing to swing. My three friends await my swing. My mind tells my arms to swing. But I can't swing. I'm petrified—stiffer than a driver with a 6.5 rifle shaft.

Over and over, the dispatcher in my brain commands, "Swing, stupid," but my arms don't get the message. That's because the message—and this isn't part of the dream, just my interpretation—is being intercepted by Fear.

I can't swing, I surmise, because I'm afraid. Afraid of the boiling water and piranhas. Afraid of failing. Afraid of disappointing my three friends, who probably couldn't care less whether I hit it 275 down the middle or shank one into the boiling water, as long as I just hit the stupid ball so they can have a turn. Afraid that after the round, friends, family, and people at work will ask how I played and I'll feel obligated to give them two numbers—three if I really stink—and if those numbers aren't low enough, I'll somehow feel inadequate, even though most of those people couldn't care less about those numbers.

So I'm immobilized by fear. I'm like Gulliver, the fairy-tale giant who gets tied down by the Lilliputians—only I get tied down, in mid-backswing, by the Fear Fleas. Thousands of them, each carrying dozens of tent pegs and hundreds of feet of worry rope, enslaving me until my alarm goes off and I awaken.

I know this all sounds a little strange, the kind of stuff you might hear from a guy on a leather couch who's talking to his golf therapist. But trust me on this one. I have this theory about life and golf and God and fear.

In essence, I believe that how we live our lives and how we swing a golf club have some similarities, particularly in terms of how we react to the Fear Fleas. And that my dream probably has something to do with my real-life fear of failure—on the course and off.

The answer, I've come to believe, is Romans 12:2: "Do not conform any longer to the pattern of this world, but be transformed by the renewing of your mind."

In golf, we get filled up by all sorts of advice, from the simplicity of "keep your left arm straight" to—I've actually seen these in golf magazines—"pretend you're pushing a child in a swing" or "pretend you're in a canoe going over a waterfall." We're so bombarded with advice that the mind isn't allowed to trust the basics that really make the swing work. The result? Fear.

Likewise, in life, we get filled up by all sorts of advice from people and organizations and advertising and books and movies and educators and political parties and lobbyists and cults and media about how we are to live. In essence, we conform to the patterns of the world, which suggest there's some sort of security in following the will of the masses, regardless of what that will might be.

We're so bombarded with "secrets to success"—tonight I saw a leaflet inviting me to a session on "conscious breathing," as if ignoring my breathing patterns for 45 years might have somehow impeded my human potential—that fear sets in. We're too petrified to swing.

Recently, I was playing a beautiful golf course in Central Oregon that sits, like a giant table, alongside the 300-foot-deep Crooked River Gorge. I had played 11 holes and each time I stood over a tee shot, I had absolutely no confidence I could hit the ball straight. And I didn't. I was scattering drives like a nozzled garden hose left unattended with the water on full.

At this point on the course, you're on the edge of the table, the gorge falling straight off to your left at a spot where we traditionally try to hammer a few balls across the abyss while waiting for slow players ahead. I teed up a ball and instinctively knew I could hit it straight, long, and pure. And did. Three times in a row, almost to the other side of the 300-plus yard-wide gorge.

Hmmm.

I then stepped to the 12th tee, stood over the ball, and immediately thought: *Trouble right. Don't slice.* And to complete the self-fulfilling prophecy, proceeded to slice a ball right into the trouble right.

The difference between the two situations? On the gorge shot, my only "target" was to hit a ball into a seemingly infinite canyon; how could I go wrong? I got to the top of my backswing and, fearing no consequences should I scrub the shot, allowed myself to swing through the ball correctly. I let go. I relaxed. I trusted my swing.

Bottom line: When I stood at the edge of that gorge, I was transformed. I renewed my mind and my body followed suit.

And when I went back to the actual course? As I faced the hole, I got to the top of my backswing and, fearing all sorts of bad consequences should I scrub the shot, I didn't trust my swing. I didn't pull through with my hips and shoulders. Instead, I swung with my arms in a subconscious attempt to steer the ball straight, to back off, to ease the ball down the fairway.

Bottom line: I conformed to my old painful patterns and my body followed suit.

Our Big Life fears come from all sorts of places. Perhaps we were raised by perfectionist parents for whom nothing was ever good enough. Perhaps we were once part of a legalistic church where punishment, not encouragement, was the order of the day. Perhaps we've experienced so much pain in our lives we don't feel worthy of happiness.

When people are fearful, they panic. In golf, their swing collapses. Later, in desperation, they buy new equipment with hopes of a quick fix to a problem that's much deeper. In life, their world collapses. And, in desperation, they head to the mall or the QVC channel or some shopping web site with hopes of a quick fix to a problem that's much deeper. In both cases, we try to rejuvenate our lives with water from the well of materialism instead of renewing our minds through the One who made us.

Regardless of what creates the fear, I believe the answer is trust. Is there a more reassuring verse than Jesus' beckoning us to "Come to me, all you who are weary and burdened, and I will give you rest" (Matthew 11:28)?

It is the essence of New Covenant Christianity: "Trust me. I'm there for you. Don't worry about the boiling water and the piranhas; concentrate on what can overcome that trouble. Me."

A while back, I was caddying for my 19-year-old son in a golf tournament. On the first hole, a par-5, I suggested he hit his second shot down the left side of the fairway so he could avoid hitting his third shot over a huge, gaping trap that guarded the right side of the green.

"What trap?" he said.

In essence, I came to realize, he has learned—i.e., renewed his mind—to ignore such trouble. In his mind, that trap didn't exist. Why? Because he knows that if he trusts his swing and hits the approach shot he's capable of hitting, the trap won't come into play. In this case, he was right: He hit his second shot down the right side of the fairway, and hit a 6-iron to within 12 feet to set up a birdie attempt.

Certainly, good mechanics are integral to a good golf swing, just as a good understanding of God's ways are integral to good living. But in both cases, it's less important what we know than what we *do* with what we *know*.

I think, for example, of people who know every nook and cranny of the Scripture but whose lives don't reflect it: people who can explain "pre-millennialism" with ease but stumble badly at "doing unto others as you would have others do unto you." It comes down to trust.

Better, I think, to trust God's deep love for us and His willingness to forgive us than to spend our whole lives trying to find some elusive Secret to the Swing.

"My grace is sufficient for you, for my power is made perfect in weakness," says Jesus (2 Corinthians 12:9).

Ah, but I've botched so many shots, some say, I'm hopeless. "As far as the east is from the west, so far has he removed our transgressions from us," writes the psalmist. "As a father has compassion on his children, so the Lord has compassion on those who fear him" (Psalm 103:12-13).

When you understand God's grace is wider than even a gaping gorge, you're empowered by endless love to renew your mind and be transformed. You're free to live beyond the patterns of the world. You step to the tee and see potential, not pitfalls.

Trap? What trap? And those piranhas and boiling water? They exist only in the nightmares of people like me who, at times, trust too little.

The Sportswriter

❖ ❖ ❖

They are the scribes. They tell us what happened and why. They score the plays. Interview the players. Describe the action for those who couldn't see it and those who saw it but want the details. They are both insiders—those who get close to the action—and outsiders—those relegated to experiencing the game vicariously, not firsthand. They are the sportswriters.

17

Dream Makers

A rocket won't fly unless somebody lights the fuse.
—Homer Hickam Jr., *October Sky*

In 1965, my fifth-grade teacher at Garfield Elementary School in Corvallis, Oregon, stood in front of the class and boldly announced that Career Day was coming. Her name was Mrs. Wirth. She had red hair, perfect cursive writing, and that sort of youthful enthusiasm that would later remind me of TV's Mary Tyler Moore.

Her eyes scanned the room as if searching for life's possibilities. "So, people," she said, "what do you want to be when you grow up?"

She then told us that each of us would get to choose someone from the community who does a job related to our field of interest. She would try to arrange for us to watch that person in action and ask him or her questions.

We had a week to decide who that person might be, but I already knew. When it was time to make our choice, Mrs. Wirth went alphabetically through the class until she came to the "W's."

"And, Mr. Welch, what would you like to do?" she asked.

At age 11, I was a freckle-faced wonder with a crew cut and enough butch wax on my forehead to mortar The Great Wall of China. I didn't know much about a lot of things, including why everyone in the world but me had a Sting-Ray bike. But I did know what I wanted to be when I grew up.

"I want to interview Paul Valenti, the Oregon State basketball coach," I said. "I want to be a sportswriter."

Mrs. Wirth looked at me and nodded one of those nods that began as surprise and evolved into affirmation.

She was a fresh-from-college schoolteacher, not some veteran miracle worker. And she held in her hands the futures of 29 kids, one of whom had just boldly asked for the moon.

Paul Valenti, meanwhile, was a major-college basketball coach in his first year of trying to replace the legendary Slats Gill. Gill had been the head coach at OSU since 1929, the year the stock market crashed. He had won 599 games and nine conference titles, and was so revered in Corvallis that they named the basketball arena after him after he retired. The pressure on Valenti was considerable.

But when a young schoolteacher called to see if Valenti would give half an hour to an 11-year-old boy, he said yes. The rest, as they say, is history, recorded on the pages of *The Garfield Chatter*, a school newspaper that published the story written by me and two buddies who helped me interview the coach.

Dreams, I've come to believe, are almost always partnerships. They require a dreamer and a dream maker; someone with the vision to go someplace and someone willing to help the person get there.

Mrs. Wirth could easily have said my request was out of reach; couldn't I choose something a bit less ambitious? But instead she made it happen. So she's among those I've always credited for helping me become a writer.

Others helped. So did journalistic genes. In 1905, my grandfather, Will Adams, not only kept an illustrated and box-scored baseball journal that ultimately wound up being given to me, but he and his pals published something called *The Hooligan Gazette*. It was a neighborhood newspaper that, amid stories on bicycle-propelled airships and alien abductions, included sports stories.

My father was a photographer and an artist, a man whose creativity showed through in pictures and drawings, in movies and Christmas cards and sketches of sailboats on the water.

At 7, my scrapbook will attest, I was already creating newspaper sports pages, almost exclusively about Oregon State University football. They came complete with orange-and-black crayon illustrations of players catching footballs that, in relation to those players, were roughly the size of the Hindenberg blimp. At 9, I had already photographed a Corvallis-Sweet Home basketball game. And at 12, I received the kind of Christmas present few 12-year-olds receive from their parents: a subscription to *Sports Illustrated*; the next year, I got a desk on which to place my Smith-Corona typewriter.

When our local newspaper, the *Corvallis Gazette-Times*, needed a representative from my junior high basketball team to phone in game results, I eagerly volunteered. The morning after each game, I would call Jack Rickard, the sports editor, and read him the final score, points for each player, and the score by quarters. After saying each name, I could hear the staccato click of his typewriter as he translated my words to paper. It was miraculous.

After getting home from basketball practice that night, there it would be: a story in the *Gazette-Times* about our team's latest loss, complete with the names and numbers I'd phoned in just that morning. Amazing!

If this job got my foot in the door, Little League baseball swung it wide open. Would I be interested, asked Mr.

Rickard, in compiling the town's baseball results for a story each day during the summer?

It was like Wendy being asked by Peter Pan if she wanted to fly. Each evening, a Parks and Recreation guy would deliver to my house the results from dozens and dozens of games. I typed those results into one long story. And because there were so many games and because I didn't want my copy to grow stale, I created a systematic approach.

I created a list of every verb I could think of that described what one team could do to another:

trim	edge	down	nip
clip	whip	trip	top
stop	drop	bounce	blank
thrash	trash	thump	crush
cream	cruise past	slip by	roll over
turn back	outslug	outlast...	

and, my personal favorite—a word that I always thought gave me such a sense of sophistication because of its length and challenging spelling—"annihilate."

Nobody in my stories ever hit a triple; they "lashed" a triple. Nobody ever pitched a two-hitter; they "twirled" a two-hitter. I wrote of 31-0 games, of Steve Schmidtz's unassisted triple play, of the Flying Saucers whipping the Astros, and the Moonblasters thrashing the Fireballs.

My first byline appeared as "Tom Welch," the kind of mistake in which the half-right factor offers little in the way of consolation. But how could I complain? I was being paid $35 a summer for something I loved to do, a hefty sum for which I felt slightly guilty.

My stories sometimes included the heroics of a wiry little kid named Harold Reynolds, who would go on to become the best baseball player my hometown would ever produce—an American League Gold Glove champion at second base for the Seattle Mariners during the '80s, and, later, a host on ESPN's "SportsCenter."

My love for sportswriting deepened. I began reading all the greats from the past, including Grantland Rice and Red Smith. Writing about four key Notre Dame players in a 1924 football game, Rice once began one of the most notable sports stories in history like this: "Outlined against a blue-gray October sky, the Four Horsemen rode again...."

I never wrote anything quite that artsy in the Little League roundups—usually, it was something more like "Tom Boubel lashed two triples as the Cobras creamed the Cheetahs 12-2 Thursday..."—but I dreamed I someday would.

I became sports editor of my junior high newspaper and then my high school newspaper, both of which were advised by a man, Jim MacPherson, who was like my Mr. Holland of journalism. We called him "Mac." He inspired us to reach for the stars—and the dictionary. What's more, when a typewriter fell out of the newspaper's third-floor office—we'd been using it to prop open a window since we were getting hot playing an impromptu baseball game in celebration of making deadline—he forgave us.

When the *Gazette-Times'* Rickard asked if I wanted to cover some high school football games, I told my folks I was going to actually be sitting in a press box, a place of such utter privilege that I scarcely believed my good fortune. A few days later, they surprised me with a new pair of binoculars.

In the summers, I started reading the masters: Ernest Hemingway and William Faulkner, John Steinbeck and Flannery O'Connor. I dutifully clipped out the monthly "Word Power" features in *Reader's Digest* and, during breaks at work on a spot-fire crew, had a co-worker test me on them. Once, on a weekend backpacking trip, I skimmed through an entire dictionary, a feat which friends still chide me about 25 years later.

Meanwhile, I went from being sports editor of my high school newspaper in Corvallis to sports editor of my college newspaper 40 miles away in Eugene, having the misfortune of serving at a time when the University of Oregon's 14-game football losing streak was the longest in the nation. By the time the Ducks finally snapped their 392-day victory drought, so few people were in the stands that, from the press box, we joked it would be faster to introduce the fans to the players than the players to the fans.

Throughout college, I worked part-time in the sports department at *The Register-Guard*, the local daily. On Friday nights, the pattern was six hours of game-watching, car-driving, deadline-hovering, story-writing, phone-answering chaos. Once, a copy editor named Paul Harvey, a gruff guy who smoked like a chimney and loved model trains, kept looking at his watch and pestering me to finish my story.

"Not quite finished," I said, tapping away on the Royal.

"You are now," he said, and literally ripped the story out of the typewriter, slapped a headline on it, and sent it downstairs to be typeset.

After my shift ended and my adrenaline ebbed, I would take the elevator to the basement, buy a 50-cent hot dog from the vending machine, put it in the microwave, and think the same thought each week: *Could life get any better than this?*

I graduated from college and became sports editor of a small daily newspaper in Central Oregon. A few years later, Bob Chandler, the publisher of the paper, took me to lunch at a place called Tony's Poco Toro, the only restaurant I've ever eaten in that had red crushed lava rock on its roof. Mr. Chandler, about 60 at the time, looked a little like actor Lionel Barrymore. From his shirt pocket he pulled out a small substance of what looked like a chocolate brownie wrapped in cellophane, took a plug, and extended it to me. It was chewing tobacco.

"Care for some?"

"Uh, no thanks."

He then wrapped it back up, stuck it in his pocket, and said, "So, Welch, what do you want to be when you grow up?"

I laughed lightly and said I was happy being a sports-writer. He listened, or pretended to, then said, "Welch, you're one of the first sports editors we've ever had who actually had an English class before he got here. You can't spell worth beans, but other than that, you know the language. You can't cover Bend High football games the rest of your life."

I took that as a compliment from a man who issued them with roughly the frequency of the Olympic Games—every four years. But still, "This is all I've ever wanted to be," I said.

"Be more," he said.

It took me awhile, but I later realized he was right. In the years to come, I would leave sports, become a features writer, then a columnist. I would start writing for magazines, then write books. And I would wind up one day at Oregon State University, giving a reading from *A Father for All Seasons,* a book about fathers and sons that I'd written after my father died in 1996.

It was, in a sense, a homecoming. This was Corvallis, my old hometown, a few hundred yards from where it all began, where I'd interviewed Paul Valenti 33 years before for the *Garfield Chatter.*

I was reading a chapter when, looking up from the book, my eyes scanned the room. That's when I saw her in the audience: a red-headed woman who looked to be in her 50s. For an instant, I hesitated, smiled ever so slightly, then continued on with my story.

As I glanced at her from time to time, her eyes said the same thing they'd said to me back in that fifth-grade classroom in 1965. Said the same thing that the other dream makers had said to me all along, whether it was through a gift of binoculars, a lesson on writing, or the simple encouragement to be more.

What that look said is: I believe in you.

Still.

The Shoelace

He was a no-name kid lost amid big-name athletes, a 22-year-old runner from Atlanta named Tim Willis who was competing far from home. He was an 800-meter guy. And he was in Eugene, Oregon, on this mild June evening in 1993 to run in the USA/Mobil Track and Field Championships at the University of Oregon's Hayward Field.

Reporter's notebook in hand, I stood at trackside. Willis's race began. As the runners in the two-lap event spaced themselves out, Willis quickly fell to the back of the pack. After half a lap, he was about five yards behind the leaders. After a full lap, about 10.

Had this been Hollywood, Willis would have run the bell lap like an inspired sprinter, lunged at the finish line to win, and later found himself surrounded by reporters and autograph seekers. He would have been the hero of the day. And when he awoke the next morning at the Hilton, the newspaper left in front of his room would have been emblazoned with his photo.

Instead, Tim Willis finished dead last. His time, 2 minutes and 10 seconds, wouldn't have won most high school meets. I watched as he sat in the infield, putting on his sweats. Not far away, reporters and autograph seekers crowded around pentathlete Jackie Joyner-Kersee.

Sometimes, courage lives in the shadows. On this night, at least, it did. On this night, it lived in the heart of a young man named Tim Willis. There is nothing particularly noteworthy, you see, in running 800 meters in 2 minutes and 10 seconds.

Unless you're running blind.

❖ ❖ ❖

He was 10 when it happened: Coats' Disease, a hemorrhaging of the retina. Within three years, Tim Willis's vision was completely gone. In junior high, he started wrestling, which required running. The high school cross-country coach saw him run and invited him to come out for the team.

Why not?

Willis learned to stay on course with the help of a shoe-string tether he shared with a guide, who ran beside him. The guide would say something like, "Ditch coming up. Three, two, one, ditch!" Tim averaged about one fall per race, but nothing worse than skinned knees.

By the time he was a senior in high school, Willis was scoring points as one of his high school's top five runners. But with him now making a difference in team results, the Georgia High School Association ruled him ineligible to run. Being tethered to a guide, they said, gave him an advantage that other runners didn't have. It broke the rules.

Willis was crushed. But after the story ran on the front page of the *Atlanta Constitution*, calls of support for Willis poured in from around the country. *USA Today* picked up the story. Willis was on national TV. And the athletic association overturned its ruling.

Tim Willis ran on in the darkness.

❖ ❖ ❖

On the day before his race in Eugene, I met Tim Willis at the university dorm he was staying in across from Hayward

Field. Reporters generally ask the questions, but instead Willis led off with one for me. Would I be willing to drive him to the spot where distance runner Steve Prefontaine had died?

Minutes later, we were there, on Hendricks Hill just east of the University of Oregon campus. I watched as Willis's hands felt the contours of a rocky wall along a narrow, twisting lane. All was quiet, except for an occasional bird chirping and the distant whir of Interstate 5.

"Pre 5-30-75 RIP" someone had painted on the rock.

I talked of how Prefontaine had been my hero when I was a young runner. Willis talked of how even though Pre had died when Tim was 4 years old, the Oregon runner became his hero, too. "What I admired about him was the way he could come back," Willis said. "After finishing fourth at Munich, a lot of people might have given up. He bounced back and set his sights on '76."

What I admired about Tim Willis was that he ran at all. Watching him race the next night, I was reminded that courage isn't measured with a stopwatch, but in one's willingness to risk. And humility to trust.

We often find ourselves alone on that starting line. Unable to see. Blind to whatever lies ahead. Destined, it might seem, to fail.

Which is where faith comes into play. Faith is more than about running in the darkness; it's about being willing to trust someone else to lead us through that darkness.

It's about dropping our pride and, in humility, admitting we can't do it on our own.

It's about tethering ourselves to the God who longs to be our guide, and letting him lead.

Faith, it seems, is born of courage. It has nothing to do with the eyes. And, as Tim Willis taught me that summer night, everything to do with the heart.

Press Box

During my first week as an official newspaper reporter, I called the local high school football coach and asked if I could come interview him the next day. He said fine.

As I drove to his house, I remember thinking that I had finally arrived. I was no longer writing Little League baseball stories with misspelled bylines. I was no longer working for the student daily between lit and poly-sci classes. I was no longer a part-timer at *The Register-Guard*, writing stories that would get ripped out of my typewriter by impatient editors.

Instead, at age 22, I was a player in the game of life—the sports editor of a small but thriving metropolis newspaper, *The Bulletin* in Bend, Oregon. (OK, a town of about 17,000 at the time, but compared with the blink-and-miss towns of Central and Eastern Oregon, a *relative* metropolis.)

I walked to the coach's door. Hearing the inner voice of my mother, I stood up straight. I adjusted my clip-on tie and rang the doorbell. This was my moment.

"Hi," I said when the coach came to the door. "I'm here from *The Bulletin*."

He looked at me and looked at my notebook. "Well, uh, thanks for stopping by," he said, "but the other carrier came by last night to collect. I went ahead and paid him."

Thus did I arrive in big-league journalism. It was like warming up for your first major league baseball game and being mistaken for the bat boy. Fortunately, things got better.

In fact, covering sports at a small-town daily was the most fun I've had in journalism. It was also the hardest work I've ever done in journalism: six days a week, lots of nights, lots of weekends, lots of stale pizza.

On Fridays in the fall, I'd work from 6 A.M. to 2 P.M. to put together that afternoon's sports section. That night, I'd cover a game, come back to the office, and take results of, say, two dozen other games over the phones with a handful of other sports nuts till about midnight. (The latter was easier said than done, especially with losing coaches, who had a tendency to "forget" to call. After a while, you learned what bars they frequented, and had them paged. Our motto: *You can run, but you can't hide.*)

When the results were all in, about midnight, we'd start turning them into stories. We'd finish about 2 A.M., stuff down a few pancakes at an all-night restaurant, and go home to catch a few hours sleep—less if we hung around to play football in the restaurant parking lot.

Then, at least for me and my assistant, it was back at 6 A.M. to edit stories, write headlines, and design pages for that afternoon's paper. (At a sister paper in Eastern Oregon, the sports editor simply brought a sleeping bag on Friday nights and spent the night on the newsroom floor.)

The half dozen sports editors from the Intermountain League were spread out across Central and Eastern Oregon, a high-desert area as large as Georgia or Pennsylvania. In my five years as sports editor, I saw these people only once, at a makeshift "convention" we held in John Day, a place so small and rustic that you half-expected Marshal Dillon to poke his head in the restaurant during our plenary session on Selecting League All-Stars. Mostly, the sports editors communicated by phone and something called the "C" wire, a clackety-clack Teletype that was to communication what a Model-T was to transportation.

A road trip in this league would often be five to seven hours long—one way. We rarely covered Friday night games on the road. But when we did, it would mean arriving back in Bend at 4 A.M. and having a story written by 6 A.M. And then, of course, designing the pages, copy editing other stories, writing headlines, and checking pages till about noon.

Summers were more relaxing. A handful of us sports staffers would sit in the bleachers at Vince Genna Stadium, covering Bend's Class A minor league baseball team while the sun slipped behind the Three Sisters mountains to the west. Between pitches, we'd throw trivia questions to part-timers Rod Hanson and John Pritchett and watch them fight over them like sharks being tossed halibut heads.

Hanson, a local high school history teacher, was The Natural, a guy who majored in baseball trivia and minored in the odd combination of Bible and '60s/'70s music. He won so many between-inning trivia contests that stadium officials banned him from competing; he didn't care, he'd just sit back and start rattling on about Ronald Reagan's six greatest sports movies or how only two people in the Bible have names starting with "F" (Felix and Festus), or how a former Mets pitcher once tried to burn down his family's back fence.

Pritchett, fresh out of high school, was The Rookie, but could match Hanson on the most meaningless of minutia. Whenever he got down in the count, Pritchett would try diverting the theme from baseball to Erich Segal's *Love Story*, the first five pages of which he had completely memorized.

It was a wonderful life, particularly after Bend, affiliated with the Philadelphia Phillies, won the Northwest League championship in 1978. I was walking out of the clubhouse after the celebration when a small pack of autograph seekers spotted me.

"Hey, are you anybody?" one of them asked.

I couldn't lie. "Yeah, I'm somebody," I said, meaning that, yeah, I had a name and social security number.

"Cool," he said, and handed me a program. I signed half a dozen autographs that night, later wondering if those kids ever tried to figure out who I was and what position I played.

As *The Bulletin's* sports editor, I had unlimited freedom to create. I did a full-page feature on nothing but foul balls. I wrote a weekly column. On occasion, thanks to Bend's reputation as a vacation garden spot, I even got to interview some big-name athletes, including New York Giants star Y.A. Tittle, he of that famous photograph of the aging quarterback on his knees, without a helmet, blood coming from his nearly bald head. And, of course, Portland Trail Blazers star Maurice Lucas, he of that infamous interview in a moving station wagon in which, engrossed in a game of backgammon with a Blazers staffer, he never once looked up at me.

That's how it was being a sports editor for a 20,000-circulation paper: just when you thought you were pretty important, you'd be reminded you weren't. Like the January night I was going to the bathroom in the locker room at halftime of a Bend High basketball game—only to have the team in the other room finish getting its pep talk and go back on the court, leaving me locked inside. I wound up climbing out a back window into the 25-degree cold and running around the school, where I had to show identification to convince the woman I was the paper's sports editor.

I took a lot of heat from my colleagues for that one, but not as much as another reporter took after he filled in for me while I was away for a few days. It was Masters weekend, and the radio was reporting that a relative newcomer to professional golf, Spain's Seve Ballesteros, was the surprise leader.

Upon returning, I asked my assistant how everything had gone. "Super," he said. "I even saved our hide on a mistake The Associated Press made."

"What's that?" I asked.

"Oh, those bozos had 'S-E-V-E Ballesteros' in a story—left out the 'T'."

My trusty assistant, of course, had the presence of mind to tell our readers that the dashing young Spaniard, *Steve* Ballesteros, was leading the Masters.

But such downers were more than offset by other aspects of my job, such as the tremendous pay: $150 a week for 60 to 70 hours of work. At first, I couldn't believe I was going to make that much for something so fun. Later, I realized fun didn't pay the rent.

My boss, Mr. Chandler, was known in newspaper circles as the last of the rough, gruff, small-town publishers. When I asked him for my first raise, I understood why.

"No," he said, leaning back in his chair and clipping his fingernails. He then proceeded to explain all the benefits I got as an employee of his company that didn't show up on my paycheck, including free parking and the yearly company picnic at Shevlin Park.

"And there's the added benefit of living in beautiful Central Oregon," he said. "I like to think that just being able to see the Three Sisters mountains on your way to work is part of your compensation."

Great, I wanted to say, but try telling that to the guy at Green-Mindt Grocery who accepts only hard, cold cash for a quart of milk, not a peek at the South Sister.

After a while, Chandler softened up and gave me a couple of raises. But I realized it was time for a change. Chandler had long encouraged me to get out of sports; when the paper decided to begin its first-ever Sunday edition, he asked if I wanted to be its editor.

Covering sports was getting a bit repetitive. Each week, coaches would say the same threadbare clichés.

If they were going into the game as underdogs: "Any team can beat any other team on any given day."

If they were favorites: "We can't look past these guys. We need to take one game at a time."

If they won: "Our guys just wanted it more."

If they lost: "Their guys just wanted it more."

If they tied: "It's like kissing your sister."

About the only coach who offered colorful quotes was the Madras High basketball coach, who would say things like "We were so cold we couldn't hit a bull's behind with a bass fiddle." Unfortunately, most of his quotes were so colorful that we couldn't print them.

The sameness of the job and the evening/weekend work were taking their toll; by now, Ryan was 4 and I didn't want to miss him growing up, so I took the Sunday editor job.

The editorial page editor, a Felix Unger sort who wore cardigan sweaters and had an office next to the sports department—or, as he called it, the "toy department"—extended his hand to shake. "Bob," he said, "welcome to the world of journalism."

Sometimes I miss those days. I would, in the years ahead, still cover an occasional sports event; while working for a Seattle-area paper, I covered the only college football game in history in which a field goal was disallowed because of excessive celebration on the part of a horse-drawn covered wagon.

Washington was playing Oklahoma in the Orange Bowl when the Sooners kicked a field goal in the final quarter to break a 14-all tie. An illegal procedure call nullified the kick, meaning Oklahoma would have to try again from five yards farther back. Meanwhile, though, the "The Sooner Schooner" was making a celebratory loop on the field. Chagrined, officials assessed Oklahoma a five-yard delay-of-game penalty. Washington blocked the subsequent field goal, the momentum shifted to the Huskies, and they went on to win 28-17.

It was perhaps the oddest moment in my journalistic career: standing in Miami, Florida, at about midnight, interviewing a college student dressed as a wagon-train boss about how he and his horses were being blamed for Okahoma losing the Orange Bowl.

But for all that I'd do in the years after my full-time stint in sports, there remained something special about those early days in Bend. When I left, my going-away present was not a gold watch, but a golf-ball retriever to pluck balls out of water holes.

An even better present was the memories I took with me of being a rookie in the hard, cold world of big-time journalism; of refereeing a 100-question trivia contest between Pritchett and Hanson whose outcome, 20 years later, is still in litigation; and of realizing I was finally somebody—and nobody at all.

Chasing the Wind

When I was 14, I woke up one Saturday morning and felt compelled to wallpaper my room in color *Sports Illustrated* photographs—right then, right that moment, as if I were being called to fulfill some sort of latent decorating destiny.

So, almost like Richard Dreyfuss in *Close Encounters of the Third Kind* when he finds himself driven to create a mud-based scale model of Wyoming's Devils Tower in his house, I began madly cutting out photographs from the two years' worth of magazines I'd saved. I took masking tape, cut one-inch strips, rolled them together, then stuck them to an old wooden snow ski that I'd bought at the Woodman's garage sale for 25 cents. My mother always wondered why I'd bought that ski—frankly, so did I—until this Saturday morning when I needed a 7-foot-long tape dispenser. Now we both knew.

You see, when I refer to "wallpapering," I don't mean that in a figurative sense. I mean that in an every-square-inch-except-the-ceiling sense. I mean that in a took-me-two-full-days-to-do-it sense. I mean that in a used-two-rolls-of-masking-tape sense.

In a single weekend and with my mother's blessing, I turned my room into a shrine to the publication that I very nearly worshipped: *Sports Illustrated*. It was a tribute to what I believed to be the pinnacle of publishing. A magazine that embodied all that was good about sports. Above all, a magazine, I hoped, that my byline would someday grace.

They were all around me, hundreds and hundreds of pictures, creatively cropped and arranged: the images of photo masters such as Walter Iooss Jr. and Neil Leifer. Images such as the Colts' Johnny Unitas eyeing a receiver behind his single-barred face mask. Kansas City's Campy Campaneris fielding a grounder. The Celtics' Bill Russell soaring for a rebound. Runner Jim Ryun rounding a curve at the '68 Olympic Trials. Coach Vince Lombardi grinning that gap-toothed smile. Skater Peggy Fleming spinning. Baby-faced Jack Nicklaus looking like a muni player in one of those silly bucket hats. Dozens of cross-country skiers gliding across a Finnish meadow. Long jumper Bob Beamon leaping into history with a world-record jump that almost defied reason. An exhausted UCLA defensive back, Bob Stiles, being helped from the field. Ali landing a punch. Arnie sinking a putt. Doug Sanders wearing a gaudy golf outfit in which everything from shoes to hat was the color of the burnt peanuts you buy at 7-Eleven.

I'd been a subscriber since age 11 when my parents gave me the magazine as a Christmas gift. My friends all wanted to grow up and be Lou Brock or Elgin Baylor or Johnny Unitas. I wanted to grow up and be Frank DeFord or Mark Mulvoy or John Underwood, writers for *Sports Illustrated*.

I marveled at how these people could take me places and show me things and move me in ways unimaginable. At how the photos took me inside the games themselves, like being in an aquarium and seeing the fish up close. At how the artists filtered spring training or summer football camp—even a boat show—through their creative minds to offer images that said so much.

In the movie *It's a Wonderful Life,* a young George Bailey is working at Mr. Gower's Drug Store when he pulls out a magazine and boasts to Mary Hatch that he's been nominated for membership in the National Geographic Society. He then goes on to tell her how someday he will explore the world.

That was me. Only in my scene, that was a *Sports Illustrated* in my back pocket and my dreams weren't of exploring Tahiti, the Coral Sea, or the Fiji Islands, but of exploring the world of sports: athletes, games, stadiums. And having a story published in *Sports Illustrated,* I figured, would be my equivalent of discovering the lost ark of the covenant: the ultimate treasure.

My first attempt came on November 19, 1967. I was 13 and grieved that the magazine had given Oregon State only one measly paragraph after my beloved Beavers had knocked off O.J. Simpson and top-ranked USC, 3-0, so I wrote a letter to the editor.

"What does it take to get a decent article in your magazine besides being a Midwestern or Southern team or USC or UCLA?" I huffed with a hint of Northwest inferiority complex.

They sent me a nice form letter thanking me for adding to the excitement of college football.

In 1971, having matured to an all-knowing 17-year-old, I wrote again, this time chastising Tennessee's athletic director for stating that long hair impedes athletic performance.

The magazine sent me a nice form letter thanking me for adding to the excitement of college athletics.

I went to college, became a newspaper sports editor, and began freelancing on the side. In my early 20s, I wrote a can't-miss first-person piece on the travails of an athlete—me—whose past was so full of losing seasons that when my junior high football team tied a game 0-0, we celebrated with pizza.

They sent me a form letter that said, in essence, not to give up my day job.

In 1987, I sent the magazine a letter decrying Marv Marinovich's attempt to turn his son, Todd, into "roboquarterback." They didn't send me back a form letter. Instead, they printed my letter. I was thrilled. But when your dream is to write an article for a magazine, having your letter-to-the-editor run is a little like playing Class A ball in Lodi, California, instead of making it to Yankee Stadium.

Later that year, the idea hit me: I could write a piece for *Sports Illustrated* on the invention of the "Fosbury Flop" high jump style. It could run just before the 1988 Olympics, exactly 20 years after Oregon State's Dick Fosbury stunned the world with his then-wacky style by winning a gold medal in Mexico City.

I had grown up three miles from the foam pit where Fosbury had perfected his backwards style. I knew the history. This story had it all: A fresh angle. Info that wasn't common knowledge. A touch of humor. And timeliness. I fired off a query letter to *Sports Illustrated*. Weeks later, an editor wrote back. I was stunned.

She loved the idea. How would $1,250 with a $250 kill fee sound? she asked. For a guy who once made $35 a summer writing Little League baseball results for a small-town daily, being offered $1,250 to write a single article for the king of all sports magazines was like being given the keys to Disneyland after spending your life teeter-tottering. And $250 even if the article were to be rejected? I'd never been promised such handsome compensation for possible failure; it was like being on "Let's Make a Deal" and knowing that even if you picked the wrong door, you'd still go home with a year's supply of Eskimo Pies.

Not that I planned on being rejected. This was my one—and, perhaps, only—chance. I signed the contract immediately and threw myself into the project. My wife and sons, then 9 and 6, didn't see much of me the next few months.

Once home from my newspaper job, I was in my office, making phone calls, and typing. Or at the Seattle Public Library, scanning microfilmed newspaper and magazine articles until, sickened by the motion, I thought I'd throw up all over 1968.

I talked to Fosbury's boyhood pals. Old coaches. College competitors. I drove 800 miles round trip to Ketchum, Idaho, where Fosbury lived, and spent an afternoon interviewing him; even wound up paying for two motel rooms for one night. (Don't ask.) Finally, I finished the article and sent it away. Weeks passed. Then came a letter from the *Sports Illustrated* editor. I was stunned.

The editor rejected the story. Too much this, not enough that; I can't even remember what she didn't like about it. But if I wanted to redo the whole piece, she might—the word "might" stood out like the neon of a hospital emergency room sign—reconsider.

I was numb. It was a warm summer evening and I was home alone with the boys. The contractual letter had made it sound like such a done deal. I'd had this fish securely in the boat; now I was looking at a letter that said three months of work wasn't good enough. A letter that said my two-decade-long dream wasn't going to come true after all. In my journal to 9-year-old Ryan, I wrote this at the time:

> A chance at the big time—gone. I cried. I didn't know what to say. Mom was gone. You and Jason didn't quite know what to do, so you went about your normal routine. Then, after about 10 minutes, you came over, threw your arms around me, hugged me and started sobbing. "Dad," you said, "I just feel so bad for you."

I refused to accept the rejection. I called another editor at *Sports Illustrated* in hopes that he would read the story and overrule her. By sheer will, I could get that story in the magazine. I could convince these people of the errors of their way. I could—"We don't do that around here," the editor said. End of conversation.

What now? Do I admit defeat or recast the whole story? I wallowed for days. Finally, I made my decision: I would rewrite the entire article. I spent two weeks reworking it, said a prayer, and dropped it in the mailbox. I wasn't particularly hopeful. Weeks later, the editor wrote back. I was stunned.

She loved it. My revisions were just what she was looking for. It would run in a few weeks, in the September 12, 1988 issue, she said. I whooped for joy.

For three straight days, I rushed to the supermarket to see if the magazine had arrived. Finally, I saw it: the Chicago Bears' Jim McMahon was on the cover, eluding a would-be tackler. And I thought: *somewhere behind Jim McMahon is my article.* After waiting nearly 25 years to fulfill this goal, my dream was unfolding. Everything around me seemed to freeze, as if the store scanners stopped beeping and the Muzak quit playing. I opened the magazine. I flipped the pages. My hands were sweaty. Suddenly, there it was: The lost ark of the covenant.

But a week later, I was in the supermarket when I did a double take: there on the magazine rack, where the Jim McMahon *Sports Illustrated* had been the week before, was a new *Sports Illustrated* with tennis player Steffi Graf on the cover.

I couldn't believe it. Just like that: I'm history.

❖ ❖ ❖

More than a decade has passed since the day that article was published in *Sports Illustrated*. When I began subscribing to the magazine, the cover price was 40 cents. It's now $3.50. Today the magazine is a multi-level mansion, a street-of-dreams special full of angles and angst. Back then it was a simple bungalow that invited you to come in and stay awhile and listen to some well-told stories.

But if life changes, it also teaches. It took me nearly a decade to learn the *Sports Illustrated* lesson, not that I spent much time actually looking for it. It came to me in the summer of 1996, after my father had died.

Hours after learning of his death, I was standing in front of the house in which I'd grown up. The same street where I'd played touch football. The same house on which the tattered basketball hoop that my father had hung was still hanging, a slightly rusty legacy of the man who was no longer there.

I was feeling empty and lost and hurt. Then, suddenly, my 17-year-old son, Ryan, was there. He put his arms around me and hugged me and said, "Dad, I don't want to lose you like you lost Grandpa."

In the end, what I learned was the difference between what lasts and what doesn't. At the memorial service for golfer Payne Stewart, who died in a plane crash at age 42, what people remembered about him wasn't so much his golf shots or flashy attire, but his bonds with those around him. Material dreams don't last; relationships become the legacy that does.

I'm thankful my article was published in *Sports Illustrated*. But it was only a temporary high. It was, as Ecclesiastes says so well, "a chasing after the wind."

What I'm really thankful for is a son who, on that summer night when his father learned his story had been rejected, hugged me, cried with me, and said, "Dad, I just feel so bad for you."

Because eight years later, on the day my father died, that same son hugged me and cried with me in much the same way, just because he hurt for me. And I was reminded how sad it would be if we spent our whole lives loving things that can't love us back.

The Fan

❖ ❖ ❖

Fans are the cheers in the stadium, the percussion to the symphony. They tell you that they bleed their school's colors. They live and die with their heroes. They care too much, of course; it's just a game. To some, perhaps more. They memorize the statistics. Anticipate Saturday's game. Analyze it for days after it's over. They are sometimes fickle, sometimes loyal beyond belief. They are the fans.

A Part of Something

O ne Saturday in October 1988, I sequestered myself in my Bellevue, Washington, rental home like a jury member in a cheap motel, refusing to allow myself to even go outside. I didn't want to talk to neighbors, watch television, listen to the radio, or answer the phone. To do so was to risk having someone tell me what I didn't want to hear.

It was a long day of waiting. Of wondering. Of wishing. But I made it. Finally, at 11:30 P.M., and with my family fast asleep, I turned off all the lights in the living room, switched on the television and did it: watched a taped replay of that afternoon's Oregon-Washington football game from Eugene, Oregon, without knowing the outcome.

I felt a little bit like a guy in a cartoon I'd once seen—a middle-aged man, alone, roasting a hot dog over a campfire, with a caption that read something like: "Milton DeFree, self-employed, holds company picnic."

But I also felt a little bit more sinister than Mr. DeFree may have felt. As a diehard Duck fan living just outside of Seattle, home of the University of Washington, I felt like a Christian holding a one-man worship service in the former

Soviet Union. I was surrounded by millions of Husky fans, whose team had beaten my beloved Ducks 11 of the previous 13 years and who looked upon us Quacker Backers with great suspicion, if not outright distaste.

Any moment, I figured, my KGB neighbor, Mr. Miller, a devout "Dawg" who might have seen the blue glow of the TV, could burst through the door, point something at me, and say: "Turn it off, Mr. Welch. I have a remote and I'm not afraid to use it."

But one's collegiate football allegiance can't be compromised by fear or runaway imaginations. Thus, I spent the next three hours in one of the strangest states of agony and ecstasy I've ever experienced—a full-grown man, smack in the middle of enemy territory, watching a televised football game in the middle of the night. Not only that, but watching a game in which, because of my sleeping family, I couldn't yell and scream when the Ducks scored, or stomp and wail when they were scored upon.

It was, well, agonizingly awesome. Oregon, which usually plays Washington tough but squanders fourth-quarter leads and loses, didn't do that this time. The Ducks won, 17-14.

At first, I wanted to call some of my fellow Oregon fans from around the Northwest, but most of them, knowing the results since about 4:30 P.M., probably wouldn't have appreciated a 2:30 A.M. reminder call.

I thought momentarily of stepping outside the house and screaming the results to the folks in the cul-de-sac, but thought better of it, realizing that someday I might need to borrow a socket wrench from one of them or have someone pick up our mail while we were on vacation. So instead, I did the only thing I could do: stood on the couch, pumped my fists in the air, and loudly whispered staccato cheers like a machine-gun with a silencer on. *Bob Welch, Duck fan, holds one-man victory celebration.*

"Fan," I must remind you, is derived from the word "fanatic," which Webster defines as "frenzied; marked by excessive enthusiasm and often intense uncritical devotion" to something. A fan, we're told, is an "enthusiastic devotee."

I am a fan. Many people are fans. By that, I don't mean we're spectators; a fan is also a spectator but a spectator is not necessarily a fan. A spectator is someone who attends a sports event in a stadium or coliseum or gym. A fan, on the other hand, is someone like a Washington State friend of mine, Doug Mohney, who taught his parrot to do cheers for his beloved Cougars.

What's more, a fair-weather fan doesn't qualify as a bona fide fan. Fair-weather fans show up for sunny home openers and bowl games, and leave early in the fourth quarter so they can beat the traffic.

Real fans are like my friend, Scott Wynant, who, while living in California, ran up a $200 bill while having his brother in Oregon hold the radio up to the phone during a Duck football game. (This happened in the pre-Internet days before you could listen to such broadcasts nearly anywhere in the world.)

Real fans are like the Washington guy I once interviewed who lived out in the wilds of the Olympic Peninsula; one Saturday each May, he would drive his truck to the top of a nearby mountain just so he could get radio reception to the Husky's spring football game in Seattle.

Real fans are like Doris Kearns Goodwin, who, in her magnificent memoir, *Wait Till Next Year*, writes of growing up in the '50s in love with the Brooklyn Dodgers. While listening to each game on the radio—and keeping a complete scorebook—she came to believe that, though she was just one little girl, she somehow influenced the outcome of Dodgers games.

She once gave slump-ridden Gil Hodges a St. Christopher medal blessed by the Pope himself, in hopes that it would help him begin hitting again. After all, she reasoned, St. Christopher was the patron saint of travel; perhaps the medal would help him "return home safely each time he went to bat."

At confession, she also revealed to a priest that she wished harm to opposing players, particularly New York Yankees players.

> "I wished harm to Allie Reynolds."
> "The Yankee pitcher? And how did you wish to harm him?"
> "I wanted him to break his arm."
> "And how often did you make this wish?"
> "Every night," I admitted, "before going to bed, in my prayers."
> "And there were others?"
> "Oh, yes," I admitted. "I wished that Robin Roberts of the Phillies would fall down the steps of his stoop, and that Richie Ashburn would break his hand."

Like Goodwin, I've always supposed that there's some sort of connection between my allegiance to the Oregon football team and the outcome of a game. I have this unsupportable theory that the Ducks play best when I'm in the stands and worst when I can't even catch a game on radio. I hatched this theory in the fall of 1988 when I went on a two-week trip to Haiti with a Christian medical team.

When I left, Oregon's football team was 6-1, ranked 20th in the nation, and was talking Rose Bowl. When I returned, the team was 6-4, unranked, and playing without their star quarterback, whose shoulder had been separated at almost the same time my plane touched down in Port-au-Prince. Rose Bowl? The Ducks lost their last five games to finish 6-6.

Of course, there have been exceptions to my theory that Oregon plays better if I'm in the stands. In 1997, I gave up the annual Oregon-Oregon State football game to attend a Family Life Conference with my wife, which scored big points with Sally. Ah, but pride goeth before a fall. The good news is the Ducks thwacked the Beavers 48-30; the bad news is that I still haven't been completely forgiven for sneaking in a radio and earplug to catch an occasional score—ironically, during the segment on husband-wife communication.

Fandom, I've learned, can be taken too far; one Christmas Day, my extended family joined us in Eugene and, as Oregon fumbled away the Aloha Bowl to Colorado, I became a regular Grinch. But when kept in perspective—when your interest doesn't become worship—being a fan is a fulfilling experience.

It connects you to something bigger than yourself. It allows you a shared experience with those around you; among my favorite fatherhood memories are of watching athletic events with my sons. And, of course, after a week of work deadlines, there's a certain devious pleasure in having the freedom to stand up and scream whenever you feel like it.

At times, of course, being a fan can complicate life. My having grown up in Corvallis (home of Oregon State) and gone to college in Eugene (home of University of Oregon) has provided some interesting conflicts, not the least of which was watching as the best man at my wedding, OSU defensive back Jay Locey, raced 94 yards down the sidelines for a touchdown against the Oregon team for which I was rooting. How do you cheer in such circumstances? Now, I find myself bi-collegial—wanting both Oregon State and Oregon football teams to win, which works for me except when they play each other.

My boyhood is still rooted in Beaver memories, the most memorable game I've witnessed being OSU's stunning 3-0 upset over O.J. Simpson and No. 1-ranked Southern California in 1967. My father and I sat together in the north end zone, rain falling, the field a sea of mud, the crowd dressed like a mass of steelhead fishermen.

Since becoming a born-again Duck fan at 18, the best game I've seen was in 1994, an Oregon-Washington battle that I watched from the 38-yard-line with my two sons.

Down 20-17 late in the game, Oregon found itself on its own 2-yard-line, facing 98 yards and the unsettling reality that in the four years he'd been the Duck quarterback, Danny O'Neil had never brought the team back to victory when they trailed in the second half, much less against a ninth-ranked team that had earlier in the season beaten Ohio State and stopped Miami's 58-game home winning streak. But on this day, O'Neil drove the Ducks 98 yards for a go-ahead touchdown.

Ah, but the Huskies countered with a drive of their own that was excruciating for Duck fans; with 1:04 left to go, Washington was poised for the go-ahead score on the Oregon eight-yard line with first down and a timeout remaining.

"That's it. They've got it. We're finished," said my older son, Ryan, almost in tears. I could barely look myself, but mumbled some fatherly line about not giving up till the game's over. The crowd had turned quiet. Having Washington drooling at our goal line with a minute left was like facing a firing squad; the outcome was pretty much settled, it was only a matter of when.

Washington came to the line of scrimmage, ready to pull the trigger. Then it happened, a defensive effort that many consider the most incredible play in the century-long history of University of Oregon football.

Despite having pummeled Oregon on the ground to get to this point, the Huskies stunned everyone with a down-and-out pass to the shallow corner of the end zone. Oregon freshman defensive back Kenny Wheaton darted in front of the receiver at the three-yard-line, intercepted the pass, and raced down the sidelines.

Most incredible sports moments last only a second or two—some not even that long—but as Wheaton passed the only Husky with a shot to tackle him and headed unchallenged to the end zone, this play seemed to last an eternity.

In the stands: bedlam. We were hooting and hollering and hugging people around us who we didn't even know. I grabbed my camera and started madly taking pictures, knowing that I had to preserve something from this day.

I've never experienced such an instantaneous reversal of emotions; later, for some reason, I kept thinking of the darkness-to-light line in "Amazing Grace": I once was lost but now am found, was blind, but now I see.

Sports, you see, aren't an extension of life as much as a microcosm of life. And as fans, you soon realize that you're more than a spectator. Win or lose, you're somehow part of it all, whether lost in the revelry of 44,159 fans in a stadium or alone in your living room at 2:30 in the morning.

The Giant Killers

It was spring, the wrong season to be standing in a college football stadium, perhaps the wrong decade as well. For it was quiet, empty, lifeless, like a body without a soul. The stadium mirrored little of the mystique that I remembered from those autumn afternoons long ago, when my pal Woody and I would race our bikes down Arnold Way, buy 50-cent tickets, and watch what we both knew was the greatest football team to ever don shoulder pads.

In 1987, I had returned to Parker Stadium at Oregon State University half-believing it would all be the same. Of course, it wasn't; twenty years is a long time. The checkerboard end zones were gone. A larger, more sophisticated scoreboard had replaced the one that once flashed the score above all scores: OSU 3, USC 0. The muddy field on which my beloved Beavers had beaten No. 1-ranked Southern California had been replaced by artificial turf.

As fans, we all have one team that stands out above the rest. For me, this was that team: the unheralded 1967 Oregon State football team that came out of nowhere to stun top-ranked Purdue 22-14, tie second-ranked UCLA 16-16, and beat top-ranked USC—with Heisman Trophy-winning tail-back O.J. Simpson—with a lone field goal.

They were called the Giant Killers.

This was more than just one team beating the odds. It was, as one player would later say, "corn-fed boys who played with their hearts" defeating America's media darlings, a team from a state whose well-tanned governor, Ronald Reagan, watched glumly from the press box.

In the fall of 1967, a season ticket to OSU games cost $16. Simon and Garfunkel were singing about feelin' groovy. And America's favorite television show was "Andy Griffith." Once, through what I was sure was divine intervention, OSU's quarterback, Steve Preece, wound up having dinner at our house; his roommate was the son of some close family friends. I unsuccessfully lobbied my mother to frame the plate on which he'd eaten.

But everything changed after that season. Nothing would ever seem as simple. Author William Manchester labeled 1968 "the year everything went wrong." Drug use mushroomed. The Vietnam War grew uglier. Anti-war protests intensified. And Martin Luther King was assassinated.

Senator Bobby Kennedy came to Corvallis to campaign for the Democratic nomination for president; my mother took me to hear him speak in front of the courthouse. A few weeks later, he was dead, gunned down in Los Angeles.

Then, in the spring of 1969, four students from my community were driving back from a state tournament basketball game in Corvallis and were killed in a gruesome auto accident, and I realized that life wasn't as safe and certain as I'd thought.

❖ ❖ ❖

I was going through a box of old newspapers one evening when I found it, sandwiched between Neil Armstrong's moon walk and distance runner Steve Prefontaine's fatal car wreck: *Incredible OSU crumbles Troy.*

What had become of the players on this team? I wondered. At 33, I suddenly had the urge to know, the urge to write about them. *Northwest*, then the Sunday magazine at *The Oregonian* newspaper in Portland, was interested in the story, so I embarked on a journey to find out. I drove hundreds of miles, interviewed dozens of players, scanned hundreds of feet of microfilm.

What did I find?

That heroes are best remembered in the context in which we first find them. That an athlete's toughest challenge is often learning to live after the cheering has stopped. And that no matter how high we put them on pedestals, athletes are, above all, human like the rest of us.

Most of the players who had come down the Parker Stadium ramp in 1967 were about 40 years old when I returned to interview them. And most had found success in the world: they were raising families, entrenched in jobs they liked, seemingly content with the past and the present.

But not all of them. Some stumbled. Some made poor choices. Some lost focus. In short, I found they were not the invincible Giant Killers I remembered from my youth.

I remember one player who was lost without the spotlight of football. No job, no relationships—he found nothing to fill the hole sports had filled and wound up as a bouncer in a bar, brawling and drinking. On occasion, he'd stop by Parker Stadium and just stare and remember. He once wrote a poem that read, in part:

> *If you pass by a stadium*
> *Some lonely night*
> *And hear a lonely voice calling*
> *Out old remembered plays…*
> *Please don't interrupt until I have*
> *Raced across the field*
> *Weaving back and forth,*
> *Hurdling opposing tacklers with*
> *My imaginary football tucked*
> *Under my arm.*

Athletes, it's been said, die two deaths—one when their career is over and one when their heart stops. It wasn't until he was 35 that the man accepted that first death, which freed him to live again.

A few of the players tried desperately to keep playing, bouncing around the NFL and Canadian Football League. But injuries and reality caught up; only one player had a substantial NFL career.

A few of the players built what, on the outside, looked to be ideal lives. One lived atop a hill, was a successful businessman, and had a wife and two teenage children. But divorce shattered his family.

A few of the players tried to replace the glory days with money. "I had the world by the tail," one told me. "At age 23, I didn't owe a dime, I had $10,000 to $15,000 in my bank account, and I was married. So what'd I do? I started dropping acid."

If some made poor choices, others had no choice at all. On the morning after OSU's win over USC, one player didn't have time to read the newspaper accounts of what is still considered the biggest victory in the school's century-plus football history. He was on a bus to an airport. His ultimate destination? Vietnam.

He came back with a Purple Heart after a Viet Cong soldier hurled a grenade while the man was on night patrol. A buddy to his side never made it out, but he did—unconscious, bleeding, his body full of shrapnel, his right eye missing.

A year later, in 1969, OSU players were warming up for spring practice when they saw a familiar-looking player emerge from the locker room, dressed in pads, ready to play. It was the Vietnam vet.

In a made-for-TV movie, the man would have returned gallantly to grandeur. But in real life, many Vietnam vets learned you can't go home again—and, in a sense, this man was one of them. With his step slowed and his vision impaired, he never played another down of football at Oregon State.

It's now been more than a decade since I revisited the Giant Killers that fall of 1987. I was skimming the newspaper obits recently when I saw the photo: it was him, the player who had gone off to Vietnam. At age 51, he had succumbed to Lou Gehrig's Disease. He was believed to be the first member of the Giant Killers team to die.

I stared at the picture and read the obit once, then again. It didn't seem possible. These guys don't die. These guys are all 19 and 20 years old. They beat all odds. They're the Giant Killers.

But, then, maybe that was the latent lesson from revisiting the heroes of my past: that not only is life not a made-for-TV movie, but the good guy doesn't always win in the end.

A decade before, I had learned that my heroes were human—and unprotected by helmets, shoulder pads, and youth, not nearly as indestructible as they appeared through the eyes of a 13-year-old. But until now, I'd never considered the ultimate Goliath: death.

Blaise Pascal, the 17th-century French religious philosopher, believed that each of us is born with a longing in his heart—a longing destined to be filled with something, or someone. It is, he contended, a God-shaped vacuum.

Athletics, I believe, can neatly fill that vacuum. For a while.

The adulation of others, I believe, can neatly fill that vacuum. For a while.

Youth, I believe, can neatly fill that vacuum. For a while.

But I don't think anything ever fits—and keeps fitting—like the One whose perfect shape is missing, the One who promises to guide us through the changes of life, the One through whom we can slay even the ultimate Goliath.

On that day in 1987 that I'd returned to Parker Stadium, it had been the campus chimes that drew me back. After hearing those bells, I remembered my father and I sitting in those end zone seats. When the USC game was over, when Goliath finally fell, we rushed the muddy field and frolicked with a bunch of players who never thought they'd ever wake from this dream and go off to war or wind up in drug rehab or be served divorce papers or die.

In some ways, I wish I could freeze-frame the fall of 1967, for it had a purity about it that's been polluted in the decades since by a culture increasingly bent on greed. By the painful realization that life buffets even the strong. And by the inevitable winds of change.

Since the fall of '67, everything had changed—and nothing had changed at all. I left the stadium. In the campus quad, the Alpha Phis were selling Candy Grams. As I drove down Arnold Way, two boys on bikes glided toward the campus and, for a moment, I watched them in my rearview mirror.

The Gift

The time you won your town the race
We chaired you through the market place;
Man and boy stood cheering by,
And home we brought you shoulder-high.
Today the road all runners come,
Shoulder-high we bring you home,
And set you at your threshold down
Townsman of a stiller town.
Smart lad, to slip betimes away
From field where glory does not stay
And early though the laurel grows
It withers quicker than the rose....
　　　　　—From A.E. Houseman's poem,
　　　　　　　To an Athlete Dying Young

I heard the news on one of those sunny spring mornings that, at least in Oregon, you wish you could Select All, Copy, and Paste to replace some drizzly January day nine months hence.

I was heading into the University of Oregon's Allen Hall, home of the School of Journalism, when a friend greeted me not with his usual hello but with a chilling question.

"Did you hear about Pre?"

"Hear what?"

"He's dead."

Steve Prefontaine, at only 24 the greatest distance runner in America, had been killed in a car accident shortly after midnight. He had missed a turn on Hendricks Hill, less than two miles from campus, and rammed his sports car into a rocky outcropping. It had flipped and pinned him underneath.

Impossible. As a sportswriter on the campus paper, I had just seen him win the 5,000 meters in a track meet the previous night. I had watched as he jogged his traditional victory lap to celebrate his 25th straight win, the crowd of 7,000 fans at UO's Hayward Field applauding their hero with "Go-Pre!" gusto.

Impossible. A week later, I was sitting in those same Hayward Field stands at a memorial for him. No victory lap this time, only remembrances of an athlete dying young. The stadium clock ran as we sat in silence; it would stop at 12 minutes and 36 seconds, a world record for three miles with which Pre would have been well satisfied.

As the seconds clicked away to commemorate this life, so did my memories of Pre....

❖ ❖ ❖

I first saw Steve Prefontaine on a cool spring evening in 1969 while attending the Corvallis Invitational track meet in my hometown. I was a junior high ninth-grader in my second year as a miler. I was a hack, a kid who'd realized he was too light for football, too short for basketball, too slow for the sprints, and yet too passionate about sports to not find some way to fit in.

Pre, three years my senior, was all that I was not: fast, gutsy, charismatic—a kid from Coos Bay, a small, blue-collar community on the Oregon coast, who was starting to run times that had race officials staring at their stopwatches in disbelief.

I remember the buzz in the stands as No. 13, the slight kid in black shorts and a white Marshfield High top, pulled away from the field that evening in the two-mile:

"...The kid has no fear..."

"...Sixty-eight-second first lap..."

"...Record pace..."

The race was the meet's second-to-last event, and the April darkness only added to the drama as Pre, far ahead of his competitors, raced the clock.

"It's within reach," somebody with a stopwatch said. "The American record!"

As Pre pushed the pace lap after lap, we realized we were in the midst of greatness—on a small high school track, a touch of sports history was unfolding before our eyes.

Down home stretch he flew, breaking the tape and collapsing into the arms of his coach, Walt McClure. Prefontaine had broken the national high school two-mile record by more than seven seconds, clocking 8:41.5. I cut out the article from the next day's *Corvallis Gazette-Times* and filed it in a manila folder marked "To Remember." Thirty years later, I still have it.

Pre would go on to complete his high school career without having lost a single race in Oregon his junior and senior years. As a college freshman, Pre made the cover of *Sports Illustrated*—"America's Distance Prodigy, Freshman Steve Prefontaine." In the photo, which I proudly displayed in my bedroom as part of my *Sports Illustrated* "wallpaper," he was shown running alone on a hill outside Eugene, overlooking the McKenzie River. He was now wearing the green and yellow of the University of Oregon, the home-state college that he'd chosen because its legendary coach, Bill Bowerman, had written Pre a note that spoke the same kind of bravado that fueled Pre's passion to succeed: if Prefontaine came to Oregon, Bowerman had hand-scrawled, he would become the greatest distance runner ever.

Therein lay the Prefontaine mystique: it wasn't just that he was a young man blessed with speed and stamina, nor even that he was an unlikely hero—a man cheered by thousands but who lived in a rusted trailer and lived on food stamps. It was that he took "The Gift," as he called it, and dared to carry it as far as he possibly could. "To give anything less than your best," he would tell young athletes at clinics and camps, "is to sacrifice The Gift."

He didn't care how unrealistic it was for a slight kid from a tiny Oregon lumber town to even think about being the best runner in the world; instead, he fixed his eyes on a dream, toed the line, and, once the gun went off, never looked back.

What he looked at was the clock. If there's an image of Prefontaine frozen in the minds of those who saw him run, it's the image of him rounding the final turn and taking an almost-panicked glance at the stadium clock on the far side of the track.

Prefontaine loved to win and hated to lose, but he seemed to run for another purpose, as if he needed to win in a place deep within himself, a place that transcended the race results, a place few of us dare to pursue for fear we might not reach it.

In addition to his desperate drive to succeed, what added to the Prefontaine mystique were the elements of time and place. As the '60s became the '70s, America was fighting two wars—one in Vietnam with bullets and bazookas, the other back home with angry words and sometimes violent anti-war protests. Amid the Kent States and Watergates of the era, Prefontaine emerged as a kid whose all-out style could take you away from four dead in Ohio and White House lies. We needed a hero; Prefontaine eagerly obliged.

What's more, he emerged in Eugene, the hallowed home of distance running, where an unprecedented 26 runners have run four-minute miles; where Olympic Trials, NCAA, and national meets have been held with regularity; where coaches like Bowerman and Bill Dellinger groomed distance runners with a sort of homespun approach that mirrored the earthiness of Oregon itself; and where Nike was born, Bowerman using his wife's waffle iron to create the first rubber soles.

Amid it all, Prefontaine reigned as this mop-haired role model for runners everywhere. At Corvallis High, on the same track where Prefontaine had burst onto the national scene in 1969 with his record two-mile, I can still remember our cross-country coach bellowing at us before a workout: "Hey, let's get ready, guys. Stretch out. You don't see Pre standing around like this."

No, what you saw Pre doing was taking off at the sound of a gun and never looking back; he simply ran away from the competition. You saw him waving to his beloved fans in Eugene, where he won 35 of the 38 races he ran. And you saw him occasionally popping off to reporters—and, at times, to spectators.

Pre was good, and he knew it. In 1973, during a dual meet between Oregon and Oregon State in Corvallis, I was sitting in the stands with a friend who went to OSU and had little love for anything related to the sinister UO. For some reason, Pre ran the three-mile that day instead of dropping down to run the mile against Oregon State's Hailu Ebba, an Ethiopian with incredible speed and stamina.

After Ebba clocked a track-record 3:58.1, my friend spouted to anyone within earshot: "It's a good thing Pre didn't race Ebba, 'cause he woulda got smoked."

"Wanna bet on that?" retorted someone nearby, only not quite that nicely. We looked down the row and there he was, Prefontaine himself, giving my friend a laser look.

At times, intensity works against people when they let it go too far; at times, Pre's ego got the best of him. After failing to set a record in a meet in California, his post-meet moaning all but blamed the citizens of Fresno for allowing there to be too much wind.

When I arrived on the Oregon campus as a freshman in 1972, Pre was among the first interviews I did for the college newspaper. It was an early-morning phone interview that won't go down as one of my more fascinating one-on-one sessions, but Prefontaine was Prefontaine: brash, impatient, and to the point.

Just like he ran. In the 1972 Olympic 5,000-meter race in Munich, Prefontaine faced the toughest field he would ever run against. At age 21, the youngest in a 13-man race, he was going toe to toe with such international greats as Lasse Viren of Finland, who had set a world record in the 10,000 meters earlier in the games.

Pre wanted an all-out race in which the winner would simply be "who's toughest." He wanted a guts race, a Coos Bay race. What he got instead was international politics, a sluggish game of cat and mouse by runners with far more political savvy than he had. Finally, with four laps to go, Pre forced the pace with 62.5-second and 61.2-second laps, far faster than the 67-pace the field was on; Prefontaine was either going to win the gold medal or die trying.

Spent after twice being rebuffed while trying to pass on the final lap, Prefontaine reached for something more on the homestretch, but it wasn't there. He struggled home in fourth place. Viren won in a time four seconds slower than Prefontaine's Olympic Trials time.

Pre was crushed. But slowly he forgot about the past and began focusing on the future. He went unbeaten as a college senior, won an unprecedented fourth straight NCAA three-mile championship, and, in the next two years, tested himself against the best international competition there was.

Now, when he came around the final corner of a race, his eyes were not only on the stadium clock, but on the 1976

Olympics in Montreal and a rematch with Viren and the others.

Alas, he died trying.

Hours before his death, he had been at a party that drew some of the national and international stars who had raced that evening. The autopsy results, after his 1973 MGB hit the rocky outcropping, would show that Pre's blood-alcohol level was 0.16, well above the Oregon legal driving limit of 0.10.

As I said, sometimes people's intensity works against them when they let it go too far. But if some are justified in shaking their heads and thinking "what a waste," if Pre's brashness sometimes went too far, his running legacy can't be ignored.

Would he have become, as Bowerman once promised, the greatest distance runner ever? Perhaps. Most runners don't reach their primes until 25; Bowerman purposely held Prefontaine back, he said, so he would peak in his late 20s.

The world will never know. Viren went on to win the 5,000 and 10,000 meters in Montreal, and to place fourth in the marathon—an incredible triple that suggests Pre may never have been the world's best. But for a hack like me—a guy whose greatest glory was a 4:59.8 mile in a meet on the same track Pre averaged 4:21 for *two* miles—Prefontaine remains an inspiration.

On most Mondays, a friend and I run across "Pre's Trail" alongside the Willamette River and through forests of firs to the top of Hendricks Hill. Our route often takes us by the rocky outcropping where Pre took his last breath 25 years ago. "Pre's Rock" it's called.

Even now, people still leave their race numbers on the rock, sometimes a pair of running shoes, sometimes a poem. Which makes me wonder: What did Pre leave for us?

I'm not sure what he left for others. But for me, what he left was something I've had in my mind's "To Remember" file for a quarter of a century: the encouragement to take "The Gift" and make of it all that we can—to fix our eyes on that dream and, once the gun goes off, to never look back.

24

David and Goliath

And David put his hand in his bag, and took thence a stone, and slang it, and smote the Philistine in his forehead, that the stone sunk into his forehead; and he fell upon his face to the earth.

—1 Samuel 17:49 (KJV)

I had just walked in from coaching a Saturday morning soccer game and was still numb from a typical Northwest drizzle when my wife handed me the phone. All I wanted was a hot shower and an afternoon to relax.

"It's Johnny U," she said—not to be confused with THE Johnny U, the Baltimore Colts quarterback, Johnny Unitas. My friend John Mills had inherited the "Johnny U" moniker back when we were growing up in Corvallis, Oregon— home of Oregon State University—because he not only wore geeky black high-tops like his hero but, like Unitas, could throw a football as if it were shot from a cannon.

Like me, Johnny U had taken a job in the Seattle area and now here he was, 13 years after our high school days, asking me to go watch lowly Oregon State get utterly humiliated by the Washington Huskies in a downpour surrounded by

60,000 fans wearing purple and gold and singing their unofficial school fight song, "Tequila," after each of their team's 12 touchdowns.

"You gotta be kidding," I said. "Have you looked outside?"

"Bobby, this is the day. This is the Beavers' day. I feel it."

"Johnny, the Beavers are 37-point underdogs."

"Trust me."

I had read the sports page that morning. It was October 19, and Oregon State hadn't scored a touchdown since September 21. In their last two games, they had lost by a combined score of 97-0. The Beavers hadn't beaten the Huskies in 11 years. They had won only one road game in the last seven years. They were on a four-game losing streak.

"Oregon State," quipped one sportswriter, "is college football's get-well card." A TV station had shown an old film clip of Knute Rockne, the legendary Notre Dame coach, and said not even he could inspire the Beavers to victory. The 37-point margin was a joke, a Seattle sportscaster said. "It should be more like 70."

OSU was starting an untested freshman at quarterback. What's more, its only real offensive threat, flanker Reggie Bynum, had a bad ankle and wouldn't play.

The Husky Machine, meanwhile, was starting to roll; Washington had won four games in a row after going 11-1 the previous year and beating Oklahoma in the Orange Bowl.

The last time Oregon State had been to a bowl game, I was learning fractions at Garfield Elementary School. The last time they had had a winning season, 1970, not only were the players on its current team not born, but those players' parents were battling pimples and getting their learner's permits.

"Mills," I said, "It's gonna be ugly."

"Trust me."

"I'm already soaked. I've been coaching soccer."

"The tickets are free."

"The traffic. I'll get stuck on the floating bridge."

"Bobby, you won't regret it."

I looked at my wife with pleading eyes that said: *Tell me I can't go. Frown hard, as if you want nothing more than for me to stick around. Ask me to clean the gutter sludge; I'd be honored to—and will gladly tackle the shower grout when I'm through, free of charge.*

Instead, she looked at me with selfless eyes that said: *Go, with my full blessing, and have fun.*

I just stood there, saying nothing. Finally, I mumbled "OK" and started to gather my rain gear, with the solemnity of a man going to a funeral.

Everyone likes a good upset: Ali over Liston, 1964. The New York Jets over the Baltimore Colts 16-7 in the 1969 Super Bowl game. The U.S.A. hockey team over Russia and Sweden in the 1980 Olympics.

We all like a good upset, in part, because deep down, it gives us hope that we can beat the odds, too. It reminds us that we can overcome. That our fate is not sealed because of a situation we were born into, a poor decision we made, a circumstance beyond our control.

All of us, rich and poor, are, in a sense, born underdogs. Perhaps not in a material sense, but in a spiritual sense. Born with a need to connect with the One who made us. Born to find fulfillment on the deepest of levels but too often settling for something much less.

Early on, Jesus was an underdog. Soon after he was born, Mary and Joseph fled with him to Egypt because King Herod wanted him dead. Wanted him dead so badly that he decreed males age 2 and younger be killed.

But he overcame. He grew up, came of age, and went to work for the other underdogs of the world.

"Blessed are the poor in spirit," he told people, "for theirs is the kingdom of heaven."

"Blessed are those who mourn, for they will be comforted."

"Blessed are the meek, for they will inherit the earth."

He healed the sick, fed the poor, gave hope to the hopeless. And said that when we do the same, we, in essence, do it for him. He chastised those whom the world looked upon as winners, the Pharisees and their pride, the rich men and their gold, the powerful ones and their arrogance.

As it was in the beginning, so did the rulers come after him in the end. But just as it was in the beginning, so did he overcome. He beat the ultimate odds against the ultimate foe: death itself.

"He has risen!" ministers around the world say on Easter morning.

"He has risen, indeed!" comes the response.

❖ ❖ ❖

When one of our cats used to catch a squirrel, it would often toy with the almost-dead animal before going in for the kill. That's what was happening at Husky Stadium in the third quarter on this drizzly October day in 1985.

An Oregon State defensive back had intercepted a pass in the end zone to stop one Husky touchdown threat. A botched snap from center by Chris Chandler—a guy who would one day go on to quarterback the Atlanta Falcons in the Super Bowl—had cost the Huskies an almost sure field goal. And another drive had stalled at the OSU 3 yard line.

Still, Washington was leading 17-14 and had the ball first and goal on the OSU one-yard line. Four chances to go 36 inches; pretty good odds for an offense. This was it. This was the cat finally giving notice: game over.

But after failing twice to score up the middle, Washington fumbled on third down and the Beavers recovered. Husky fans started doing something Husky fans rarely do: booing their own team. A sprinkling of fans in orange and black, including Johnny U and I, went nuts.

As we watched from our end-zone seats, we quietly basked in the newfound respect the Husky fans seemed to be according us. Losing to the Huskies by only a field goal would mean we could walk out of the stadium with heads held high.

The game wore on. Washington managed a field goal in the fourth quarter to make it 20-14 and, later, with just under two minutes left, prepared to punt from its own 20-yard line, right in front of us.

I always remember the play in slow motion: defensive end Andre Todd bursting through the line on the right side...the punter receiving the snap from center...Todd smothering the punt, the ball caroming off him into the OSU end zone, bouncing around like a leather lottery ticket, awaiting the lucky taker...OSU's Lance Northington swooping in and pouncing on the ball to tie the game 20-20... Oregon State's players piling on the two heroes in celebration.

Moments later, Jim Nielsen's PAT kick sailed through the uprights. The scoreboard showed 21-20, a score that would be on the board at game's end and seared into the memories of Beaver Believers forever.

"Hey, thanks for the ticket," I said to Johnny U as we headed to the parking lot.

"What'd I tell you, Bobby? You gotta trust me."

Washington would go on to win the Freedom Bowl that year. Oregon State, meanwhile, would go on to lose its next eight games in a row. As I write, the Beavers haven't beaten Washington in the 14 years since that drizzly October afternoon. But every now and then, when looking for socks in a dresser drawer, I come across an orange and black "I Was There" button commemorating the 1985 victory, and I'm reminded that David once rose up to defeat Goliath, that no odds are too great, that the meek shall inherit the earth.

The Father

❖ ❖ ❖

Fathers are the guys sitting in the stands, quietly going crazy. They wonder if the coach is doing the job, if the ump is doing the job, if their son or daughter is doing the job. They're the guys out back, playing catch, remembering what it once was like when they played catch with their father. Or why their father never took the time. They revel in the successes, try to be philosophical about the failures. They are the fathers.

25

Trinity

The world is never again as it was before anyone you love has ever died, never so innocent, never so fixed, never so gentle, never so pliant to your will.

—Roger Kahn, *The Boys of Summer*

What I remember most about my father, even though he wasn't a huge sports fan, was this trinity: he and I and a game. And as I look back, what I appreciate most is a subtle selflessness in this man for whom sports never meant as much as they did to me.

I remember Sunday nights, playing "knee football" in the living room. With my father on his knees and me standing my tallest, we were about the same height. The football was a pair of bundled-together socks from his middle-upper drawer.

The rules were simple: If I made it to the couch it was a touchdown. I never played defense. I just took the socks and ran at my father as hard as I could, trying to reach that couch, over and over—and he would bounce me back like the flippers on a pinball machine, over and over. Then, just when he realized I was about to burst into tears because of

my lack of success, he would, with an Oscar-worthy performance, allow me to slip past him and dive into the couch,
the roar of 41,000 fans rocking the house.

I remember him hanging the basketball hoop above the
garage—and what a strange shot he had, a lightning-quick
release, like one of those lizards with the killer tongues. But
he rarely made a basket.

I remember going to bed with a promise that in the
morning, the dorky red plastic football helmet that Kenny
Shepard had given me would be magically transformed into
a Los Angeles Rams helmet, complete with those ever-cool
horns. And when I awoke, it was there, like magic, the result
of my father's late-night artistry. Nobody else on the entire
planet, I figured, had such a cool helmet.

I remember street football on Saturday mornings, before
our friends the Wisslers would arrive to go with us to
Oregon State games, my father wearing wingtips and
throwing "bombs" that got only halfway to their intended
destination.

I remember waiting for 3 P.M. one summer day, a time
that I never thought would come. My father and I were
driving two hours to Portland to see my first professional
baseball game—not a major league game, but a Class AAA
game—with my uncle. When we arrived in Portland, it
started raining. The game was canceled. I was crushed. But
my father suggested we go to a movie called *It's a Mad, Mad,
Mad, Mad World* in a huge theater downtown unlike anything
back home, and I thought it was the funniest movie I had
ever seen and forgot all about the game being rained out.

I remember him giving me the baseball journal that his
father had given to him, and how at first I shrugged it off as
some insignificant part of a man I never really knew—and
how as I became a father myself, I suddenly realized it was a
treasure: short descriptions of sandlot baseball games my
grandfather had played in, back in 1905 in Portland, accom-
panied by self-designed box scores and sketches of the action,
including first baseman Harry Young stretching for a wide

throw with the caption: "Harry always was a natural born reacher."

I remember a pitch-and-putt golf course a friend and I set up in the woods beside our campsite at Cultus Lake. A much-yellowed scorecard showed I shot 31-31—62 to win a six-man tournament pitting The Young Golf Pros against The Old Wise Mouths. My father finished last with a 37-40—77.

But you see—he *played*. He willingly became part of my world, even if he had no natural affinity for it himself.

I remember this guy off to the side of the cross-country course or the baseball diamond or the football field, squinting into a movie camera, its lens focused on me.

I remember a generation later, the same man, off to the side of my son's baseball games, squinting into a camera, its lens focused on one of his grandsons.

I remember him growing old and, after decades of hearing him gently remind me to buckle up, hearing myself gently reminding him, for the first time, to buckle up.

I remember the phone call from my sister saying he had died. It happened in a cabin we had rented up in the mountains to celebrate his and my mother's 50th wedding anniversary. It was on a golf course lined with pines, beside the second hole.

Now, whenever I play that hole, I see that house and think of my father and want to make par, maybe even birdie—for him, to somehow honor him. Then I remember that he never really cared if I made pars or birdies or won the race or scored 20 points or caught the winning touchdown pass. He only cared that I was out there, enjoying the challenge, giving it my best, having fun, taking that pair of socks and diving past him, into the couch, with the roar of 41,000 fans rocking the house.

And I realize that the best way I can honor my father isn't to accomplish things. The best way I can honor him is to simply be the kind of father to my sons that he was to me.

The Big Leagues

In most parents' life, a time comes when their child finds himself thrust into the real world, girded for battle by years of parental guidance, ready to test his skills amid the turbulence of an ever-changing world.

It's called t-ball.

Here's the journal of my younger son's first season, during which he started on a team called the Pilots. He was 5:

April 30. Across town, the Seattle Mariners' motto this year is "Anything Can Happen." They picked the wrong team. Do Mariners players ever pretend their gloves are Halloween masks? The Pilots do. Have the Mariners ever gone two weeks without making an out? The Pilots have.

This is a team full of imagination, spunk, and candor. Unfortunately, the only out the Pilots made today was when a grounder caromed off the second baseman's right ankle and accidentally rolled in the glove of the first baseman. Indeed, anything *can* happen—and does.

"Good job out in the field," one mom said to her son-the-center-fielder as the Pilots readied to bat. "Next time, remember your mitt."

With 18 kids on the team and a coach who looked like he'd rather be on a highway litter patrol, there wasn't much action today. In 75 minutes, my kid took two swings at the ball and fielded one grounder. I brought my video camera. I should have used time-lapse photography.

May 7. The season has hardly begun, and already the team has been racked by controversy. Apparently the Pilots' coach went off and got married, and his honeymoon went into extra innings. He's gone.

"Who cares about the coach?" says one mom. "My kid just wants his uniform."

The Pilots got their uniforms, but not my kid. In a surprise move that rocked the sports world, he was traded to the Cougars, an expansion team. There was no press conference. Nobody speculated about the terms of the agreement. Instead, the coach just said, "You, you, you, and you—come with me." They ought to try that in the major leagues. It would be much simpler than the drawn-out contract negotiations.

The Cougars are a lot like the Pilots in that their outfielders sometimes play with their backs to the plate, and their infielders get easily distracted, say, if someone in the stands blinks. When a ball comes their general direction, however, all 13 of them pounce on it like seagulls on crab bait. One kid fielded a grounder and tried to throw it to first. A teammate jumped up and blocked it.

So far, the biggest challenge for these kids seems to be making the transition from batting to going out in the field. When the two teams switch positions, it's like the changing of tides—it takes about half an hour and there's an undercurrent of confusion.

But the fans love it. One mother was so engrossed in the game she spent two innings reading a *National Enquirer* that included an article about a horse that can drive a 1960 Lincoln Continental. For a while, that peeved me. But later, after the paper blew my way and I took a look at the article, I understood her fascination. Butterscotch—that's the name of the horse—can even honk the horn!

May 14. Depending on who you talk to, the Cougars either won 21-3 today or lost 17-5. I couldn't figure it out. One of the coaches actually tries to keep a scorebook on these games, a job slightly more difficult than charting the daily movement of all the salmon in Puget Sound.

How, for example, do you score a play in which all three right-fielders muff a grounder, one of them finally throws it to the first baseman, who tries to catch it with the back of his left ear since he's busy watching a hot-air balloon in a nearby parking lot; the left-fielder's dad tosses the ball back on the field to the shortstop, who throws it to the pitcher, who throws it to the catcher, who tags out a player—only to find it wasn't the kid who hit the ball in the first place but the next batter up?

May 21. I couldn't help but notice today the different "ready" positions the players use while playing in the field. The three most popular seem to be:

—The Mitt Face. When the umpire yells "batter up," the defensive player puts his mitt over his face and peers through the finger gaps. This is perhaps the most versatile defensive position in that, besides preventing sunburn, it guards against dirt bombs being thrown by mischievous infielders.

—The Hand in Pocket. This position seems to work perfectly—until the player has a ball hit to him. Then, when his hand gets struck, he's forced to throw opposite-handed or throw the ball with his mitt—always a favorite with the crowd.

—The About-Face. In what must be an apparent attempt to psyche out the batter, the infielder turns around and faces away from the plate. Not normally an effective way to scoop grounders, but great for balls that bounce off the legs of out-fielders employing the Mitt Face or Hand-in-Pocket method.

June 4. What's the lost-ball penalty in baseball? The Cougars beat the Trail Blazers—or at least that's what all the Cougars said—in a game featuring exactly that. Maybe the stars were all aligned just right or the Cougars were all aligned just wrong or the outfield grass was a bit too long. Whatever, somehow a Trail Blazer batter hit a ground ball into the outfield that nobody on the Cougars ever saw. Finally, after getting directions from coaches and parents, the team found the missing ball in left-center.

June 11. The season ended today with a game against the Bombers. I must admit, there's been improvement. Those grenade throws of April have lost at least half their rainbow arc. Rarely do more than two runners find themselves on the same base at the same time anymore. I even noticed that the Cougars' shallow left-center-fielder—we have about a dozen outfielders—is remembering to wear his glove.

Not that there's not work to be done. Today's highlight came when one of the Bombers stole first base. I mean literally stole first base.

Turns out he was only using it as a Frisbee.

The Dying Light

Do not go gentle into that good night.
Old age should burn and rave at close of day;
Rage, rage against the dying of the light.
—Dylan Thomas

I line up the six-foot putt. All is quiet, save for a few people talking quietly in the distance. Slowly, I take the putter back and stroke the ball. For a split second, the ball rolls toward the hole, then slides decidedly off to the right, like a car exiting a freeway long before its destination.

"Maybe you'd like to try something else," says the young salesman, watching from beside the artificial-turf putting green.

For an instant, our eyes meet. I am standing in one of the West Coast's largest golf shops and a young man 25 years my junior is telling me—behind his veneer of entrepreneurial etiquette—that I cannot putt.

After 32 years of golf frustration, it's time, I've decided, to face the reality that I can no longer blame my ineptness on my irons or woods. Instead, I've decided to blame it on my putter. So here I'm shopping for a new one. After nine years, I am kissing my Northwestern Tour model good-bye for a younger, sleeker model.

I feel so cheap; alas, I am a desperate man. At 45, my golf game is going through a mid-life crisis. And so it has come to this: a belief, a hope, a desperate clinging to the idea that I can somehow buy my way back to respectability.

Long a believer that the swing, not the equipment, makes the golfer, I've scoffed at friends who plunk down hundreds of dollars to find "new-and-improved" clubs to help them once again hit the drives of their youth. I've chided them for seeing some pro win a tournament, then rushing out to buy the replica of the putter he used; after Jack Nicklaus's stunning Masters win in 1986, who can forget that rush on those putters whose heads were roughly the size of bricks? The golfer makes the club, I've long insisted; not the other way around.

But in recent years, my game has gone so far south that even my putter talks with a twang. Blame it on a schedule where golf now makes only a rare guest appearance; after months of not playing, I usually prepare for a round like I prepare for a yearly dental checkup: by flossing the night before—i.e., hitting a bucket of balls, and hoping I can fool the hygienist. Of course, it never works—in the dental chair or on the golf course.

Blame it on a number of other excuses; the bottom line is that some saleskid who didn't even start shaving until after the invention of the Big Bertha driver is now trying to help save my golf game.

I look up at the kid with one of those don't-you-think-I-know-what-I-need looks on my face, then put my pride on a leash. "Sure, let's try something else."

"If you'd like, you can go out on our real putting green and test them," says the young salesman.

The kid is nice—he's only trying to help, after all—but something about this situation just doesn't seem right. I take three putters, a couple of balls, and start walking toward the outdoor putting green.

"Uh, I'll need you to leave your driver's license," he says.

"I'll only be, like, 200 feet away," I say.

"Store policy."

You gotta be kidding. What's he think I'm going to do—take three putters and a couple of Titleists and hop the first plane to Mexico?

"Seriously?" I say, thinking that my slight balking will probably wave the mandate.

"Sorry."

I look at the young man incredulously and say the only thing that's left to say.

"But I'm your *father*. Doesn't that count for something?"

"Sorry, store policy."

I pull out my driver's license and hand it to the kid who I once taught to drive. The kid I once taught to play golf. The kid who I haven't beaten on a golf course since he was a sophomore in high school.

I love this kid. I'm proud that, at age 20, he's found himself a job that he likes and is good at. I think it's wonderful that he has developed into a near-scratch golfer who has shot 69, won back-to-back men's club championships, and posted an 84 at night, using a glow-in-the-dark ball.

But deep inside I have this tiny dream: to beat him just one last time, at anything: golf, home-run derby, or h-o-r-s-e on the backyard hoop. Like Nicklaus coming back to win the Masters at age 47, I'd like one last hurrah to remind the world I'm still around.

It's not a vindictive thing at all. It's just a little pride thing. Not a chest-beating thing, but Pride Lite. Father-son pride. It's wanting to be the hero one last time. It's wanting to still be considered significant, like when you give your son a bit of advice about life itself and he tries it and it works and you think: I'm still needed. I still matter.

And one more thing: weird as this may sound, fathers want their son's approval. In Ryan's journal, I wrote this about the first time we played golf together as a team. He was 16:

> Going to the 18th, the two teams were all even. I nailed a 152-yard 7-iron to within two feet of the cup, sunk the putt for birdie and we won! But I was so nervous standing over that putt, more nervous than you'll ever know. (Until now.) Why? Because I wanted so badly to prove to you that I wasn't just this hacker of a dad. That I could pull through. That I could produce under pressure. Because I want you to be the same kind of guy, whether the venue is golf, marriage, work, whatever. I want you to pull through when you need to. Withstand the pressure.

"Do you wanna try one of these putters?" he asks, snapping me back to reality. "This is like the putter you bought me when I beat you for the first time."

I remember the day. He was 15. I shot 88. He shot 86. Though I'd done all I could to prevent it, I was glad he'd won. Proud to have been outdueled by my own son. I wrote a mock newspaper article—"Ryan stuns Dad for first win!"—and made good on a promise to buy him the putter of his choice.

Since then, it's been his show; I've watched proudly from the edges of the fairway. And learned what it must be like for a kid to grow up with high-achieving parents, because whenever I play now, people expect me to be good because Ryan is. And I'm not.

Not long after Ryan won his second men's club championship at a Eugene public course, I teed up my opening drive at the same place and promptly hit it out of bounds. It was like Einstein's father flunking Algebra I.

"So," said the starter, "you're Ryan Welch's father, huh?" As if he really wanted to say, "So much for that axiom about the acorn not falling far from the tree, huh?"

For the most part, I've accepted this role reversal. Twice now, Ryan has had me caddie for him in tournaments that brought together all the winners of club championships from around the state. And I've considered it one of the highest honors a father could be accorded: to be able to carry on my back the clubs of a son I used to carry in my arms.

But deep down, the instinct quietly gnaws at me to prove myself—to nobody else but myself.

That instinct welled up on a recent Fourth of July. A bunch of families from our church had gathered at the home of our friends the Schars, whose large front yard and the growing twilight begged for a game of Wiffle ball.

Naturally, two teams were divided: Youth vs. Old Codgers Who Can't Even Change a Light Bulb Without Being Sore the Next Morning. It was humiliating. The punks were hitting balls so high the FAA was probably picking them up on radar. Our outfielders were forced to play so deep we were in a small orchard, next to a barn.

Then came the True Moment. It was, we had decided, the final inning. Two outs. I was playing right field and Ryan was at bat. He drilled a hot grounder my way. I made the stop and instinctively readied to fire it to second, then realized Ryan was nearly already there.

In a split second, I realized what was happening: he had no intention of stopping. He was going full bore, intent on stretching a routine single into a home run. He was doing what 20-year-olds instinctively do when competing against their fathers in front of a crowd of people, including their girlfriends: trying to humiliate their fathers with an in-your-face touch of arrogance that I would have done myself 25 years ago.

I could have thrown the ball to third base and hoped for the best, but Wiffle balls, sometimes with even a breath of wind, can sail away like Sky King's plane at the start of his old TV show, just as the announcer says "Brought to you by Nabisco!" What's more, in games like this, the team at bat provides the catcher, and so it's not uncommon that they "accidentally" drop the ball when trying to make the tag or "accidentally" sprain an ankle just before the ball arrives.

I knew what had to be done. As Ryan neared second, I locked my eyes on home plate—actually, home rag—and, ball in hand, headed for it like a bird dog on a bead. I was going to single-handedly make this out.

My teammates would think I was crazy; the play called for a throw to second or third. But they didn't know my son. They didn't know me—the deep, mid-life me. True, this was Wiffle ball, not golf. But at age 45, you take your opportunities where you can find them. This was my Don Quixote moment to dream the impossible dream…to fight the unbeatable foe…to right the unrightable wrong, i.e., that youth should somehow get the last laugh.

About the time I crossed the base path between first and second, Ry was swinging wide around third base and hot dogging his way home in front of the two dozen spectators.

We were two generations on a collision course, the Road Runner and Wile E. Coyote with plans to outfox one another; father and son on missions for the ages.

At the pitcher's mound, I felt my first sense of hopelessness. He was too young, too fast, too committed to succeed—and only about 15 feet from reaching that success. But in every athlete's mind there comes a split-second when you must decide whether you will absolutely lay yourself flat to win or give something less. In that split-second, I didn't care if this was just a pick-up game at a Fourth of July picnic; I was going for it.

I tilted forward like a sprinter preparing to break the tape— perhaps too far forward. I started to stumble and lose control, my feet unable to keep pace with my desire and ego. Had I been an F-15 trying to land on the USS Teddy Roosevelt, the air boss on the radio would have been screaming: "Pull up! Pull up! You're coming in too hot. Pull up!"

But it was too late. I was either going to tag this kid an instant before he touched home rag or crash and burn trying. For the first time, Ryan glanced left and realized he wasn't trying to beat the ball home, but his father carrying that ball. Momentarily, he eased up, as if to suggest he was going to hammer home this humiliation like one of those oh-so-cool football players who, moments before hitting the end zone for a certain touchdown, slows down to mock the defender.

Then, when he realized I actually had a chance to make the play, his eyes filled with fear, like a horse spooked by a rattlesnake.

Six feet from the rag, Ryan dove with all he had. Six feet from the rag, I dove with all I had. I reached out in mid-air and strained to touch the ball to his back just inches before his hand reached home. We both went sprawling, Ryan heading south, me heading south-southwest. No umpire was around to yell "safe" or "out" but everybody knew the truth: I had nailed him. The kid was out.

Fans and players alike whooped and hollered. The two of us got up, a crazed man who still thought of himself as a boy and a wild boy who thought of himself as a man. Both of us drenched in sweat. Both of us huffing and puffing—one of us a bit more than the other.

Our eyes met. He gave me a small nod, then a hand slap. Though he'd done all he could to prevent it, he seemed somewhat proud that I had won this dual of the decades. Proud that his father had the gumption to beat the odds. And him.

Weeks later, at the golf shop, I returned from the practice putting green to where that same young salesman was waiting.

"I'll take this one," I said, showing him the putter I had chosen.

He handed me back my driver's license, then started waxing poetic about some kind of Big Bertha 3-wood. I had no intention of buying a 3-wood; equipment is overrated. The golfer makes the club; not the other way around. But by the time I walked out of the store half an hour later, I'd not only bought the putter and that 3-wood, but a 5-wood as well. (What can I say? The kid is a good salesman.)

We said good-bye. Ry headed off to help another customer, to continue his quest of making his own way in the world. New clubs in hand, I headed off to the driving range, to rage against the dying of the light.

The Homemade Trophy

In 1989, professional golfer Mike Reid stood on the brink of winning one of the game's major championships—the PGA. He had a commanding advantage with only three holes left; like a stock-car racer with a huge lead, all he had to do was keep his car on the track for the final lap and the title was his.

But he couldn't. He bogeyed the last three holes and lost by a stroke. Reid was crushed. He flew home to Provo, Utah. There he was greeted by his family, including his oldest child, Brendalyn, then 8. She was holding something in her hand: it was, he realized, a homemade trophy. She handed it to him. On its side were inscribed these simple words: "No. 1 Dad."

Sometimes it's the innocence of a child that reminds us of the purest form of love: unconditional love.

Unconditional love is love that asks nothing in return. In a marriage, it doesn't require a prenuptial agreement. In a church, it doesn't require a tally sheet. In a parent-child relationship, it doesn't require an if-then clause.

It is love that demands nothing. Love with no strings attached. Love that perseveres despite the circumstances. It is also the most difficult love to give, particularly in the realm of sports, where so much is based on the very thing that unconditional love is not: performance.

I was keeping score at a fifth-grade basketball game when a mother rushed to me when it was over. She desperately had to know how many baskets her son had made. Curious, I asked why.

"We pay him 25 cents per point," she said.

I can understand an occasional financial reward for an outstanding report card. But intentional or not, what message—whether it's true or not—do we send to our children when we pay them per basket? Simple: that they are only worthy when they succeed. Never mind the more subtle message offered by the bucks-for-baskets approach—that the only thing valuable in basketball is scoring. (What, nothing for a solid game of defense? An unselfish assist so someone else might score? Great support from the bench?) What it really says is that there is a hidden tally sheet, there is an if-then clause, there are strings attached.

"Love," says 1 Corinthians 13, "is not self-seeking, it is not easily angered, it keeps no record of wrongs."

I'm a realist. I understand that in the business world, the person who sells the house gets the commission; I understand that the child with the high GPA and SAT scores gets the college scholarship. But in a time when children are aching for validation of their worth, we need to offer that validation based not on what they have done but on who they are—God's creations, worthy for their simply *being*, not their *doing*.

For parents, sports are a double-edged sword. We revel in our children's performances; what parent hasn't felt the pride of seeing his or her child score a goal or knock in a run or skate a strong routine? But we also can punish our children—if even through such subtleties as distancing ourselves from them after a game—when they've not met our expectations.

Only 10 weeks after he turned 18, my older son won the men's club golf championship at the public course where he worked on the driving-range crew. He had chipped in for an eagle on the first sudden-death playoff hole against a former NCAA Division I player. I watched as he walked forward to receive his plaque in front of a group of guys mainly my own age. I was proud of him.

But two years later, that same son walked into our bedroom at 1 A.M. and, nearing tears, said, "I just wrecked my car." While reaching down to pick something off the floor, he had veered into a curb, wiped out two mailboxes, and done $1800 worth of damage to a car that had cost only $1500. Nobody was hurt. But I was not proud of him.

If, as a parent, I love my child more because he won that golf tournament and less because he wiped out a mailbox stand, my love is conditional.

"Love always protects, always trusts, always hopes, always perseveres," says 1 Corinthians 13:7. "Love never fails."

Yes, I believe parents should revel in their kids' successes. Better yet, we should revel in our kids, period. Last summer, my younger son was on a baseball team that played about 50 games. One of his teammates, a pitcher, played in perhaps ten of those games—even then, perhaps for only an inning or two of relief. But his mother never missed a game.

That is unconditional love. That is a mother who's saying to her kid—even though he may not hear it until he's a parent himself: "I love you even when you're only keeping the pitching stats. I love you even if your ERA looks like a really good gymnastics score. I love you even when you give up a grand slam, miss a catcher's sign, walk the No. 9 batter. I love you even when your coach berates you or ignores you. I love you, period."

There's a difference, you see, between loving our kids at performance level and loving them at gut level. Between loving them where they're at, and where we wish they were at. It's easy to support a kid when he's meeting our expectations; the challenge is supporting a kid when he's not.

It angers me when I see a coach in a youth game march to the mound, grab the ball out of the pitcher's hand, and wave in a reliever—with disgust on his face. I'm not opposed to pitching changes; they're a necessary part of the game at that level. What I'm opposed to is the insensitive way they sometimes are made. No pat on the back. No "we-all-have-those-days" words of encouragement. No concern for a kid who already feels humiliated in front of his teammates and the crowd.

When a manager just grabs the ball and casts the pitcher aside, what that says to a kid is simply this: Your worth to me is totally dependent on your ability to throw a baseball. I care about you only for what you can do for me. Whatever affection I have for you can, in the time it takes to throw one wild pitch, disappear just like that—snap.

In essence, it says the opposite of 1 Corinthians 13. It says love is easily angered, it keeps a record of wrongs. It *sometimes* protects, *sometimes* trusts, *sometimes* hopes, *sometimes* perseveres; it all depends on the circumstances.

Last spring, I noticed a familiar-looking young man, maybe 30 years old, at one of my son's high school baseball practices. It was, I later realized, Todd Marinovich, a former NFL quarterback. A friend of his had once attended the same high school my son attends and, along with some other adults, they were engaged in a friendly game of home-run derby while players shagged balls in the outfield.

As I watched him take his cuts, I thought about this young man who once graced the cover of *Sports Illustrated* because of his football, not baseball, prowess. I've never seen a more tragic example of conditional love than the relationship Todd Marinovich had with his father.

Marv Marinovich, an ex-pro football player, raised Todd with one goal in mind: to make him a superstar quarterback in the NFL. He conducted actual ball-tossing drills in his son's crib. He put his son on a regimented practice schedule as a pre-schooler. He brought in sports psychologists to work with Todd as a grade-schooler and a nutritionist who put Todd on a special diet.

Marv got the results he sought: Todd became a prep All-American, a freshman starter at Southern California, a No. 1 draft choice of the Oakland Raiders. But he later flunked out of the NFL, got involved in drugs, went to jail, and was last seen trying to revive his career on a Canadian Football League team.

The tragedy is not that Todd couldn't cut it in the NFL. The tragedy is that he couldn't cut it with his father. The tragedy is that a father's demands cost the son his childhood. The tragedy is that after the great experiment failed, the father never saw the errors of his ways, never had the courage to begin anew with his son—in fact, began the same process with a younger son.

Sometimes those athletes with the most talent are the ones most susceptible to conditional love. I think of a man I know—once one of the top high school tennis players in California—who could win a match 6-0, 6-1 and his father's first words would be, "So, what happened in that last game?" Nothing was ever enough.

Our children will fail. We will fail. As parents, if we can accept that as an opening premise in our lives and in the lives of our children, we're halfway home in our quest to love our kids unconditionally.

That doesn't mean we shouldn't set high expectations and help our kids to achieve those expectations; the movie *October Sky*, in which a coal-mining father tries to ground his younger son's dreams to build rockets, shows how expecting too little from our kids can hinder them, too. But the parent who doesn't allow his or her child to fail is the parent whose love for that kid always comes with a hidden agenda, a hidden agenda that may haunt that child into adulthood.

Likewise, the parent who pushes a child too hard isn't doing what's best for that child. Instead, that parent is supporting a selfish desire to live vicariously through the kid.

James 1:19 speaks of our need to be "quick to listen, slow to speak, and slow to become angry." At times, that means understanding that our children might have interests that aren't our interests. Do we love them enough to support them—or is our love conditional, i.e., only available if our children pattern themselves after ourselves?

A few years ago, my younger son began playing the bass guitar. I neither shouted for joy nor took a reciprocating saw to his amplifier; what I did was simply try to tune out this new hobby. To pretend it wasn't actually pounding upstairs as I tried to write downstairs. To hope, like a nagging cold, it would just somehow go away.

One night, I'd been asked to speak to the youth group at our church and, before I was on, the youth band played. There, for the first time, I listened to my son play his bass guitar as part of a band. In a single moment, I saw the bigger picture. I saw all that I had been missing. I heard him, through music, praising the God of the universe and I thought: *Wow. That's my kid.*

I was humbled. I realized I'd been just like that father in *October Sky* and had done nothing to encourage this interest of my son's. After we were home, I told Jason that. I apologized. I told him I was proud of him. The next morning, I found a note in my briefcase from Jason, a guy who doesn't leave many notes.

It said I'd done a "great job" on my talk and that he was proud of me, a note whose subtle message was probably "Thank you so much for not embarrassing me like I thought you might." But I took that note and pinned it to my bulletin board because I had never had a note like that from him.

What had prompted it? My willingness to listen to my son, to appreciate my son, and to share my feelings with my son.

What it comes down to, I've realized, is loving others as God loves us: unconditionally. It's grace. It's making an allowance for others' shortcomings. It's God loving us enough to send His son to die for us even though we may not only disappoint Him, but defy Him. "Father, forgive them, for they do not know what they are doing...."

It's loving our kids no more when they've made a game-winning hit, loving them no less when they've struck out, and listening to them even when the bass music isn't our idea of a sweet sound.

It's a little girl presenting her father with a homemade trophy not because of what he has done, but because of who he is: "No. 1 Dad."

And it's a father who, decades later, keeps that trophy in his display case, along with the other, less important, ones.

Final Inning

I've always thought September, not January, should be the start of the year because it's a much more pronounced time of transition. Change is much more easily discerned in first-day-of-school photos and cooler days and the beginning of football season than the minor modifying of life that January brings.

Which is why I was feeling slightly melancholy as the last summer of the millennium wound to an end; the world around me seemed to be changing faster than I wanted it to.

Some of the changes were only mild irritants:

That they had changed the name of Oregon State's Parker Stadium, where I'd grown up watching my beloved Beavers, to Reser Stadium after a $5 million donation.

That they had changed the Oregon football uniforms so the players look like a bunch of paratroopers wearing black dress socks.

And that Ryan and Jason, just before we were to take the family photograph we'd put off for years, once again bleached their hair so blond they looked like lightbulbs that get extra bright just before burning out.

But what really bothered me were all the expectations I'd had of spending time with those two boys and how few had been met. An ascent of the 10,047-foot Middle Sister had been downsized to a backpacking trip, then a camping trip, then evaporated altogether. A planned Father's Day round of golf—just the three of us—never happened because of work and baseball conflicts. And the annual playing of the 7-mile-long golf hole we build on the beach each year—by sticking a coffee can in the sand with a seaweed flag in it—was scrubbed when Ry and Jason arrived at the beach cabin without golf clubs, nor any interest in getting up at 6 A.M. and whacking a ball down the beach for three hours. (What's wrong with kids today?)

After some contemplation, I've realized it was my own fault. Why? Because I expect too much from—and appreciate too little—the time we *do* have together.

I need to accept that this father-son stuff is no longer as important to my sons as it is to me; at 20 and 17, they have girlfriends and commitments and cooler things to do than hang out with Dear Old Dad. And when I remember myself at age 20 and 17, I understand why.

It's the way things must work if we're going to allow our children to grow up and be independent of us, and dependent on God. It's what, as parents, we're made to be: the rocket booster that propels the shuttle headed for outer space, then plummets into the obscurity of the Atlantic Ocean.

It's all rooted in the "letting-go" stuff that I thought I had under control back when I wrote *A Father for All Seasons* but, like a nagging case of poison oak, keeps reminding me that I'm not over it yet. Three years later, I sat in our kitchen nook on a late-August night, talking to a fellow father about this complicated game of simultaneously letting go of our children and wanting to hold on to them forever.

"It's like this," he said: "One of our hands is pushing our sons away, telling them to grow up and build a life of their own. The other hand is pulling them back, asking them to never grow up, to never leave."

That was it exactly, this strange dance of dadhood: one minute my son is deflecting my advice as if he were back-handing a Ping-Pong ball; the next minute he's saying how much he needs me. One minute, he's all grown up, ready to take on the world by himself; the next minute, I'm helping him replace a little old lady's mailbox stand after his car wiped it out. One minute, I'm thinking how I rarely can stay awake waiting for the boys to return home; the next minute, I'm thinking back to the joy I felt when I'd return from a day's work and the two of them would come scampering to welcome me home.

Thus did we arrive at Labor Day weekend, both a welcome and worrisome bridge between two seasons. After a Friday night dinner—one of the few times all four of us had actually broken bread together this summer—I was clearing the table when I looked out the kitchen window and saw Jason standing by himself, rubber ball in hand, as if he were on the pitcher's mound in a major league ballpark.

He shook his head to his make-believe catcher as if to say, "No, not the curve, let's go with the change-up." He nodded his head yes when the catcher gave the sign he wanted. He eyed the target, began his windup, arched, and fired hard against the back of the carport wall.

Whatever happened to Rosebud, that little 4-foot kid who was terrorizing the Backyard Baseball Association just yesterday with his line drives into his mom's rosebushes? Now he was nearly my height, and growing stronger each day. But he hadn't lost something I've always loved about him: his childlike imagination.

"Ry," I said to my other son, who was also in the kitchen, "Check this out."

Ryan watched with me as his younger brother, standing in a stadium of 50,000 fans but not realizing his father and older brother were amongst the spectators, threw another pitch. Then Ryan reached for his own imagination.

He walked outside and grabbed a broom-like bat from the back shed. "OK, Jase, let's see what you can do against a real hitter," he said.

A devious smile creased Jason's face. In the last five months, he had played about 75 high school and American Legion baseball games while his once-feared big brother was lounging around a wimpy golf course. Challenge accepted.

It had been probably five years since any sort of baseball had been played in this backyard; the plywood scoreboard we'd made lay abandoned on the side of the house. Cobwebs clung to the too-small catcher's equipment and basket of balls in the shed the boys once used as a locker room.

Ryan flopped down an old rubber home plate. Jason walked as far back in our small backyard as he could get without scraping his knuckles on our cedar fence during his delivery.

Sally, carrying a plate of apple crisp and ice cream, took a seat on the deck and watched. Instinctively, I grabbed a mitt and a kids' catcher's mask that hadn't been worn in years, and crouched behind home plate. Though barefoot, I was still wearing my khaki pants and dress shirt from work.

"What's this?" said Ryan, noticing I was in the starting lineup.

"Don't forget," I said, "I was—"

"I know, I know: You were a Midget League All-Star catcher," he mimicked.

Jason's first pitch shot past me like an F-15 at an air show. Ryan swung and missed. Behind me, the ball popped a fence board loose from its lower nails. I gulped.

What followed was a half-hour of spirited father-son competition, a strange concoction of fun, fierceness, fellowship, machismo, pride, and sharply barbed one-liners. The pitches were coming so fast that I was bailing out with regularity, trying to catch them like a tap dancer waving his straw hat off to the side as he exited the stage.

The banter intensified. Sally grabbed a camera. I got the feeling that we were in the midst of something special, though I wasn't quite sure what.

With a broom bat, rubber ball, and only 35 feet between batter and pitcher, the advantage was definitely to the guy throwing. Ryan was hitting a few lazy grounders off his younger brother and managed a hard hit that would have been long gone had our towering fir not fielded it. Jason, switch-hitting, was ripping some sharp shots off the left-field and right-field fences.

Me? In four trips to the plate, I'd had one tick-foul. I was getting roundly chided for swatting at air and, while on the mound, for throwing pitches so wild that two soared into our neighbor's backyard and one almost beaned a cat. Once, I accidentally hit Jason with a curve ball that, like most of my curves, didn't.

"Don't worry," he deadpanned, "I didn't feel a thing."

My humiliation was growing. I finally reached for a card I often played back in the days of the now-defunct BBA: the bluff card. The card that says: If you can't be any good, at least act like you're good. It's a little like the magician who gets your attention with his left hand so you'll forget about what's in his right; if I could divert these guys' attention, they might forget how really pathetic I was.

I unbuttoned my work shirt and flung it into the third-base rosebush, er, dugout. I flexed my muscles in a pose I'd seen Mark McGwire do in one of those "Got milk?" magazine ads, noticing that my body might go better in a "Got fat?" ad. I dug in my feet and looked intently to the world beyond the left-field fence and the street to Effie's duplex.

The words of the P.A. announcer, sounding surprisingly like me, echoed across the stadium: "NOBODY...*nobody*...nobody...HAS...*has*...has...HIT ONE...*hit one*...hit one...OUT OF THE...*out of the*...out of the...PARK...*park*...park."

By now, the lone spectator was so intrigued by her husband at bat that she was watching geese overhead as they flew south for the winter.

Jason, who had won a few American Legion games on the mound that summer, rocked and fired. I swung as hard as I could.

"Real close," said Ryan, throwing the ball back to his brother.

Jason fired again. It was low but I went for it anyway, knowing such a pitch, if met, would go high and far.

"You're golfing," said Ryan, throwing the ball to Jason with a well-worn phrase I'd used on the two of them in BBA days.

I winced a bit because, during my follow-through, I had felt my wrist pop. For a nanosecond, I thought maybe it was God sending me to the showers or, better yet, a decent excuse to quit and end the humiliation with at least a semblance of dignity. But nobody hurts their wrist simply swinging a broomstick bat. I held up my hand to signify timeout. I dug my feet in the grass, touched the plate with the broomstick, cocked the bat, and waited.

This was it. I was going after this pitch no matter what. The windup. The pitch. At first, I thought the ball was going to hit me square in the face, then I realized it was curving. It was high and inside—one of those career-ending pitches—but I'd already committed so I swung that broomstick as hard as I possibly could, partially out of self-preservation.

Suddenly, I felt something I'd never felt on this evening: contact. Connection. Bat on ball.

The rubber ball lofted lazily into the summer sky beyond the left-field fence and seemed to gain a peculiar momentum as it rose. At first, I was thinking it would land in the street, then perhaps on the porch of Effie's duplex, then realized a frightening possibility: the ball was heading for her second-story bedroom window.

My gosh, at age 45, at a time when I should have been inside reading about retirement plans or doing a crossword puzzle, I was going to break a little old lady's window playing backyard baseball with my almost-grown sons. But just as we all braced for the crash, the ball cleared the top of the duplex like a plane in one of those Alaskan bush-pilot movies that narrowly clears a peak.

This was not just a home run, I realized, it was an Effie Ball, the ultimate, the *pièce de rèsistance* of backyard baseball. It was an upper-decker. A homer for the record books that hit the roof and probably bounced into Effie's backyard.

Having few opportunities to gloat these days, I milked the moment for all it was worth, though Jason thought I'd gone a bit far when I later retrieved the ball and gave it back to him—autographed and dated (September 3, 1999).

Despite my bravado, I later realized that the home run wasn't what had meant so much to me. It wasn't that my sons' middle-aged padre had somehow proven he could keep pace with the little boys he once purposely lost to so they wouldn't get discouraged.

What had meant so much was that:

...after two decades of parenting filled with this fascinating mixture of pride, privilege, and pain, in which I'm cheering my sons victories one moment and pulling the splinters of a mailbox stand from a Nissan grill the next...

...after a season of life in which my father's death still blindsides me now and then like a squall from nowhere...

...after a summer of spending so little time with the sons who have long since outgrown this backyard field and who, I realize, have nearly outgrown me...

...after all this, what mattered most was that as I rounded third base, two boys with wonderfully bleached-blond hair were there, as they were long ago, to welcome me home.